Whoff Whoff! And a big welcome to the Dog English Book! I hope you enjoy learning all the fun, new and interesting ways to speak to your loyal dog in English. Enjoy!
Whoff Whoff!

멍멍! 강아지영어 책을 찾아주신 것을 환영합니다!
당신의 귀여운 강아지에게
즐겁고, 새롭고, 재미있게 말할 수 있는
모든 영어 표현을 배워 보세요.
즐기세요, 강아지영어!
멍멍!

"Beauty without vanity, strength without insolence, courage
without ferocity, and all the virtues of man without his vices."
- Lord Byron

"아름다움을 가졌으되 자만심이 없고, 힘을 가졌으되 오만함이 없으며,
용기를 가졌으되 포학성이 없고, 인간의 모든 미덕을 가졌으되 그 악덕이 없다."
– 바이런 경

About the author

Matthew Douma grew up in a small rural town in Southern Canada. Ever since his early childhood years, Matthew has been in the company of pets and animals of all sorts.

Being an avid hunter, enthusiastic outdoorsman and adventurer, Matthew was rarely seen anywhere outdoors without his canine companions.

In addition to traveling, Matthew enjoys hunting, mountain climbing, sailing and writing as hobbies.

Residing in Seoul with his lovely wife Sun Hee and daughter Ennik, he works as an English education consultant and author of English educational material. This is his fourth publication.

매튜 다우마는 캐나다 남부의 작은 시골 마을에서 자랐다. 유년 시절부터 애완동물을 포함한 여러 종류의 동물들과 함께 생활했다.

열렬한 사냥 애호가이자, 정열적인 스포츠맨이며 모험가인 그는 밖에 나갈 때마다 항상 애완견을 데리고 다녔다.

그는 여행 외에도 취미로 수렵, 등산, 요트 타기, 글쓰기 등을 즐긴다.

그는 현재 사랑스러운 아내 선희 그리고 딸 에닉과 함께 서울에 거주하면서 영어 교육 컨설턴트 및 영어 교재 집필 활동을 하고 있다. 이 책은 그의 네 번째 저서이다.

Acknowledgments

Special thanks to: Sunny, Ray Rose, Jay, Christa, Alex, Judy Aran, Ahmi, Tatjana, Young Jae and Cleo for all of their valued contributions and insights that made this book possible.

이 책이 출판될 수 있도록 값진 조언과 도움을 준 서니, 레이 로스, 제이, 크리스타, 알렉스, 주디 아란, 아미, 타차냐, 영재, 그리고 클리오에게 특별히 감사한다.

*지은이를 도와 번역하신 분
설혜란 서강대 영문과 및 이화여대 통번역대학원 졸업, 현재 설통번역센터 대표.

DOG ENGLISH

강아지와
함께하는 신나는
영어회화

매튜 다우마 지음

서프라이즈

For Ennik, Emma and Lark.
에닉, 에마, 라크에게 바칩니다.

In loving memory of Buck,
the best friend a young boy could ever wish for.
어린 소년이 바랄 수 있는 가장 좋은 친구였던 애견 벅을 추억하며.

Preface

머리말

This book is intended to be an entertaining educational tool for non-native English speakers for better communication and understanding towards dogs.

The chapters in this book cover diverse aspects of dog owners and dog interactions through conversational phrases and commands. Supplementary sections dealing with bonding, training, amazing facts, and dog trivia, as well as, idiomatic expressions, which have been incorporated with an entertaining flare to keep readers amused.

As an added bonus, I have included a special section of true canine stories, accompanied with reading comprehension questions and new vocabulary lists to aid when viewing.

Filled with humorous annotations, comical quizzes, and interesting facts throughout, this book is a must for anyone who owns a canine or simply loves the company of dogs!

Matthew Douma

이 책은 재미있게 영어를 배울 수 있도록 만든 교재로서, 비영어권 사람들이 애완견과 영어로 의사소통하면서 그들을 더욱 잘 이해할 수 있도록 의도한 것이다.

이 책은 애완견과 주인 사이에 일어날 수 있는 다양한 상황에서 개에게 말하거나 명령하면서 상호 작용하는 내용을 다루고 있다. 또한 독자들의 흥미를 유도하고 재미를 돋우기 위해 개와 친해지기, 개 훈련시키기, 개에 관한 놀라운 이야기 및 개에 대한 재미있는 상식을 포함하고 있으며 'dog'가 들어가는 관용 표현도 함께 수록했다.

아울러 개에 얽힌 실화도 실었으며 그에 딸린 독해 문제와 어휘 해설을 덧붙였다.

이 책은 전반에 걸쳐 개에 대한 재미있는 설명과 퀴즈 그리고 흥미로운 사실들을 다루고 있다. 따라서 개를 키우거나 개를 사랑하는 사람이라면 특히 한 번쯤 읽어 보아야 할 필독서이다.

매튜 다우마

 contents

차례

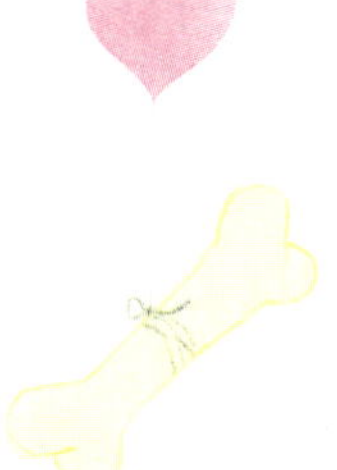

❷ Train Your Dog 애완견 훈련시키기

⑤ Dog Idiomatic Expressions

'dog'가 들어가는 관용적 표현

Appendix: The Author's Recommendation

By human standards, domesticated dogs don't do all that much. They sleep, eat, and play before going back to sleep again. Giving your dog daily love and attention, along with dialogue and playful interaction, will add excitement to your dog's life and stimulate its senses. So, enliven your dog with smothering affection and English dialogue!

인간의 기준으로 볼 때 애완견은 하는 일이 거의 없다. 그들은 자고, 먹고, 놀고, 또 잔다. 애완견에게 말을 건네고 재밌게 상호 작용하면서 매일 애정과 관심을 보인다면, 애완견의 삶에 즐거움을 더할 것이고, 또한 애완견의 감각을 자극할 것이다. 그러므로 사랑을 듬뿍 주고 영어로 말을 건네며 애완견을 생기 넘치게 해주자!

1

Speak to Your Dog

애완견에게 말하기

1 When I Meet My Dog

아침 인사

Although you may not realize it, you haven't had an interaction with your dog for several hours, so it is important to speak to your pet with a cheery voice and a chipper attitude to start the day off right. Here are the most common phrases used when an owner meets his or her dog in the morning.

잘 모를 수도 있겠지만, 애완견과 대화를 나누지 않은 지 여러 시간 지났으므로 하루를 시작할 때 애완견에게 밝은 목소리와 다정한 태도로 말을 거는 것은 매우 중요하다. 다음은 주인과 애완견이 아침에 마주칠 때 가장 많이 사용되는 표현들이다.

Good morning!
좋은 아침!

How are you?
오늘 기분은 어때?

Do you have to go outside?
밖으로 나갈래?

How's my pooch?
우리 강아지 안녕?

Do you have to go pee?
쉬하러 갈까?

Did you have a good sleep?
잘 잤니?

You must have been tired.
피곤한가 보구나.

You were snoring last night.
간밤에 코 골면서 자더라.

You were whimpering in your sleep.
Did you have a bad dream?
자면서 낑낑거리던데, 악몽이라도 꿨어?

Wow! That was a big stretch.
와! 기지개 한번 시원하게 켜네.

You look handsome.
멋있네.

You look pretty.
귀여운걸.

You're a good dog, aren't you?
착하구나, 그렇지?

Are you a happy dog?
행복하니?

You look excited.
기분이 아주 좋아 보이네.

Let's go!
자, 나가자!

2

When I Meet a Stranger's Dog

남의 애완견과 인사하기

Meeting a stranger's dog without your pet can be an interesting experience. One thing to remember when meeting a dog for the first time is that if you smile, not to show your teeth. Even a calm dog may interpret this as baring fangs and want to attack! Below is some of the most common dialogue used when meeting someone else's dog. You must always ask for permission before touching the dog. Don't forget to ask if the dog bites!

자신의 애완견이 곁에 없을 때 타인의 애완견과 마주치는 것은 흥미로운 경험이 될 수 있다. 강아지와 처음으로 만날 때 기억해야 할 한 가지는, 미소를 지을 때는 치아가 보이지 않게 웃어야 한다는 것이다. 성격이 온순한 강아지조차도 치아가 보이게 웃으면 자신을 공격하려는 것으로 해석하고는 덤벼들려고 할 것이다. 다음은 다른 사람의 강아지와 만날 때 사용되는 일상적인 대화이다. 강아지를 만지고 싶을 때는 사전에 항상 주인의 허락을 구하도록 한다. 강아지가 사람을 무는지도 반드시 물어본다.

You have such a nice dog.
멋진 강아지를 가지고 계시네요.

What kind of dog is it?
강아지 품종이 어떻게 되나요?

What breed of dog is it?
혈통은 어떻게 되나요?

How old is your dog?
몇 살이나 됐습니까?

Is it a he or a she?
수컷이에요,암컷이에요?

Does he bite?
물기도 하나요?

Can I pet him?
쓰다듬어 주어도 될까요?

Thank you.
감사합니다.

Hello doggie. What's your name?
안녕 아가야, 이름이 뭐니?

That's a wonderful name.
멋진 이름이네.

You sure are handsome. (male dog)
정말 잘생겼구나.

You sure are pretty. (female dog)
진짜 예쁘게 생겼네.

You like to lick my hands, don't you?
내 손을 핥아 보고 싶구나, 그렇지?

You have such a nice coat.
털이 정말 멋지구나.

Does your dog do any tricks?
어떤 재주를 부릴 수 있나요?

Can I see one?
한번 볼 수 있을까요?

Wow! Your dog is smart!
와! 댁의 강아지는 영특하네요!

Thank you.
감사합니다.

Good-bye doggie.
아가야 잘 가.

3 Basic Commands around the House

기본 명령

On average, dogs have a vocabulary of about 30-45 words, some dogs may have much more. Of course, some animals are smarter than others. An important factor to keep in mind when communicating with your dog is simplicity, so commands are used most often. Depending on the tone of your voice when you give a command, your dog may react differently.

개는 평균적으로 30~45개 정도의 단어밖에 모른다. 어떤 개들은 그보다 훨씬 더 많이 아는 경우도 있다. 물론 어떤 동물들은 다른 동물들보다 더 영리한 경우도 있다. 그러나 애완견과 대화할 때 명심해야 할 중요한 사실은 간단하게 말해야 한다는 것이다. 따라서 명령어가 자주 사용된다. 명령어를 구사할 때 목소리 톤에 따라 애완견은 다른 반응을 나타낼 수도 있다.

Sit!
앉아!

Stay!
그대로 있어!

Go!
가!

Come here!
이리 와!

Get up!
일어나!

Stand up!
일어서!

Get out of there!
거기서 나와!

Go lie down!
가서 얌전히 있어!

Get down!
내려가!

Go see!
가서 확인해!

Drop it!
내려 놔!

Let go!
놔!

Get 'em!
물어!

Sick 'em!
물어 버려!

Attack!
물어!

Down!
내려가!

No!
안 돼!

Be nice!
얌전히 굴어!

Heel!
바짝 따라와!

Go get me the newspaper and my slippers.
신문하고 내 슬리퍼를 가져와.

4 Doggie Accessories

애견용품

The vocabulary below is an attempt by the author to list the most commonly used dog accessories for your pet. Practice this vocabulary with your pet anytime when you use an accessory. Your pet may need to hear the vocabulary several times before he or she can remember it.

아래 용어들은 애완견을 위해 가장 많이 사용되는 애견용품 목록을 작성해 본 것이다. 용품을 사용할 기회가 생길 때마다, 해당되는 용어를 강아지에게 사용해 보라. 그 용어를 애완견이 기억하려면 수차례 반복해서 들어야 할지도 모른다.

Collar 개 목걸이	**Comb** 빗
Dog leash 개줄	**Brush** 브러시
Dog chain 개줄 체인	**Hair dryer** 헤어드라이어
Dog tags 애견 인식표	**Shoes** 신발
Dog whistle 호루라기	**Hairpin** 머리핀
Name tag 명찰	**Scarf** 스카프
Vaccination tag 예방 접종표	**Hair ribbon** 머리끈
Sweater 스웨터	**Necklace** 목걸이
Raincoat 우비	**Nail polish** 매니큐어
Life jacket 구명 조끼	**Ball** 공
Dog bone 뼈다귀 장난감	**Frisbee** 원반
Chew toy 장난감(개가 이빨로 물거나 씹는 장난감)	**Doll** 인형
Toothbrush 칫솔	**Blanket** 담요

Nail clippers
손톱깎이

Pillow
베개

Cap
모자

Backpack
배낭

Sunglasses
선글라스

Dog dish
개밥그릇

 5 Dog Emotions

애완견의 감정

Although you may not know it, your dog has many emotions and feelings. It has been estimated that some dogs have up to 100 different facial expressions. After you begin to bond with your dog, you will be able to identify the many emotions that he or she has. Below is a brief list of some dog emotions and feelings for you to communicate with your pet.

모르고 있을 수도 있겠지만 애완견도 다양한 감정과 느낌을 가지고 있다. 어떤 애완견들은 최고 100가지의 얼굴 표정을 지을 수 있는 것으로 추정된다. 일단 애완견과 서로 친해지고 나면 그가 지닌 다양한 감정들을 파악할 수 있게 될 것이다. 다음은 애완견과 대화시 사용할 수 있는 감정과 느낌에 대한 표현이다.

You look happy.
행복하구나.

You look sad.
슬픈가 보구나.

You look bored.
지루한가 보네.

You look worried.
걱정이 있구나.

You look scared.
무서운가 보네.

You look nervous.
긴장되나 보네.

You look surprised.
놀랐나 보구나.

You look cold.
추워 보이네.

You look hot.
덥나 보네.

You look sleepy.
졸립구나.

You look excited.
기분이 아주 좋구나.

You look hungry.
배고픈가 보네.

You look lonely.
외로운가 보네.

You look depressed.
기분이 가라앉아 보이네.

You look cross.
심술 났나 보구나.

You look angry.
화났나 보네.

You look jealous.
질투하나 보네.

You look curious.
궁금한가 보구나.

You look upset.
속상한가 보네.

You look serious.
심각해 보이네.

You look tired.
피곤한가 보구나.

You look confused.
어리둥절한가 보네.

Are you jealous?
질투하니?

Are you upset?
심란하니?

Are you in love?
사랑에 빠졌니?

Don't be angry.
화내지 마.

6 Dinnerfime

식사 시간

The dialogues listed below are most commonly used when speaking to your pet during a feeding. Although you may not know it, you are bonding with your pet while you feed it. Be sure to speak to your four-legged friend whenever you give him or her food.

아래 대화들은 애완견에게 먹이를 주면서 말을 건넬 때 가장 많이 사용되는 문장이다. 아직 모르고 있을 수도 있지만, 먹이를 주면서 강아지와의 유대감이 쌓이게 된다. 강아지에게 먹이를 줄 때마다 다정하게 말을 건네도록 하라.

Are you hungry?
배고프니?

Are you thirsty?
목말라?

You look hungry.
배고픈가 보구나.

You're drooling!
침 흘리는 거 좀 봐!

Don't growl at me!
나한테 으르렁거리지 마!

Is it time for your food?
밥 먹을 시간이니?

Here boy, it's dinnertime.
애야, 저녁 먹자.

Here girl, it's dinnertime.
애야, 저녁 먹어라.

It's your favorite!
네가 좋아하는 거네!

You like that, don't you?
그것 좋아하잖아, 그렇지?

Would you like a treat?
맛있는 것 줄까?

You eat too much junk food!
넌 정크 푸드를 너무 많이 먹어!

Can you smell the food?
음식 냄새가 나니?

You're hungry, aren't you?
너 배고프구나, 그렇지?

You're thirsty, aren't you?
너 목마르구나, 그렇지?

Eat!
먹어 봐!

Enjoy!
맛있게 먹어라!

Wait!
기다려!

No jumping!
뛰지 마!

Don't eat so fast!
급하게 먹지 마!

Are you full?
배부르니?

Had enough?
배불리 먹었어?

You ate too much!
너무 많이 먹더라!

You're getting fat!
너 점점 살찌는 거 같아!

You need to go on a diet!
살 좀 빼야겠다!

No begging!
음식 달라고 하지 마!

Don't eat like a pig!
돼지처럼 먹지 마!

You are slopping water all over the floor!
사방에 물을 질질 흘리고 있잖아!

You can't eat that, that's my food!
그것은 먹으면 안 돼, 그건 내 거야!

You have to eat doggie food!
너는 개밥을 먹어야지!

7 Playtime

놀아 주기

Playtime is also important to further the bonding process with your pet. Whenever possible, include direct discussion with your dog and involve him or her in activities at home. Below are some basic conversational phrases that owners have with their dog.

함께 놀아 주는 것도 애완견과의 친밀감을 강화시키는 데 중요하다. 가능하다면 애완견과 직접 대화하고 집에서의 활동을 함께 하라. 다음은 강아지와 놀 때 활용할 수 있는 기본적 표현이다.

Let's go play!
놀러 가자!

Do you wanna play?
같이 놀까?

Let's wrestle!
레슬링해 볼까!

You like to play, don't you?
놀래?

You are a playful dog.
너 놀기 좋아하는구나.

Go get your ball!
공 가져와!

Do you want to play catch?
공 잡는 놀이할래?

Do you want to go to the park?
공원에 갈까?

Go get your Frisbee!
원반 가져와!

Catch it!
잡아!

Jump!
점프해 봐!

Bring it here!
여기로 가져와!

Drop it!
내려 놔!

Let go!
놔!

Good boy!
잘했어!

Good girl!
잘했어!

Where are your toys?
네 장난감 어디 있니?

Do you want a new toy?
새 장난감 갖고 싶니?

Don't eat your toys!
장난감을 먹지 마!

Don't slobber all over your toys!
장난감에 침 좀 묻히지 마!

Go chase the cat!
고양이 잡아!

Don't chase that, it's your tail!
그것 좀 그만 쫓아, 네 꼬리잖아!

Do you want to play with your friends?
친구들과 놀고 싶니?

Play nice!
얌전하게 놀아!

No fighting!
싸우지 마!

Time to go home.
집에 갈 시간이야.

8 My Loyal Dog

Eight thousand years ago, stone-aged people tamed dogs to aid in hunting and to protect their families. It is your dog's natural ability to be loyal and devoted. Many pet owners choose to reward their dog's faithful behavior with kind loving remarks and to smother their pet with affection and praise, whenever they have proven to be loyal. The list below contains phrases that are most commonly spoken to loyal, faithful pets.

8천 년 전, 석기시대 사람들은 개들을 훈련시켜 사냥하고 가족을 보호했다. 개들의 충직함과 헌신은 본성이다. 주인들은 애완견들이 믿음직스러운 행동을 할 때 상냥하고 사랑스러운 말로 보상을 하고 숨도 못 쉴 정도로 꽉 껴안아 애정을 표현한다. 그리고 개들이 충성심을 보일 때마다 칭찬해 준다. 다음은 애완견이 충성심이나 믿음직스러운 모습을 보일 때 자주 사용되는 표현들이다.

You are a loyal friend.
너는 충직한 친구야.

You are my best friend.
너는 나의 가장 좋은 친구야.

I love you.
사랑해.

Give me a kiss.
뽀뽀해 줘.

Give me a hug.
껴안아 줘.

Watch over the house while I am gone.
내가 없는 동안 집 잘 봐.

Thank you for watching the house.
집 지키느라 수고했어.

You look sad when I leave.
내가 나가면 슬픈가 보구나.

You look happy when I come back.
내가 집에 오면 기쁜가 보네.

You follow me everywhere.
어디든지 나를 따라오는구나.

You are the only one that never complains to me.
니만이 나에게 불평하지 않는구나.

You listen to everything that I say.
너는 내가 말하는 모든 것을 잘 듣지.

You are a great guard dog.
너는 훌륭한 경비견이야.

You're my trusty dog.
너는 정말 믿음직스러워.

You trust me, don't you?
나를 믿지?

Wait here until I come back.
내가 돌아올 때까지 여기서 기다려.

Guard the house.
집 잘 지켜.

Watch over the kids.
애들을 잘 지켜.

Thank goodness you were here.
여기에 있어 줘서 고마워.

What would I do without you?
너 없이 내가 뭘 하겠어?

9 Exercise

Exercise is also a good part of the bonding process when done regularly and routinely. Whenever possible, try to include your animal in as much discussion as you can during exercise. It will help your dog to keep focused. Allow your pet to explore things on his own as well. Although playtime can be a kind of exercise, too, regular time out for walks is best to keep your pet healthy. Below are some phrases used when exercising with your pet.

운동을 규칙적이고 정기적으로 하는 것도 때, 가능한 애완견에게 말을 많이 시키는 움이 된다. 또한 애완견이 자기 방식대로 종의 운동이기는 하지만 규칙적인 산책은 다. 다음은 애완견을 운동시킬 때 유용하게 친밀감을 높이는 효과적인 방법이다. 운동할 것이 좋다. 애완견의 집중력을 높이는 데 도 물건을 찾는 것을 허용해라. 노는 것도 일 애완견의 건강을 유지하는 최선의 방법이 사용할 수 있는 표현들이다.

You need some exercise.
너는 운동이 좀 필요해.

You need to go on a diet.
다이어트를 해야겠구나.

You don't exercise enough.
운동이 충분치가 않구나.

You are getting fat!
너는 살찌고 있어!

You're too fat!
넌 너무 살쪘어!

Let's go for a walk.
산책 나가자.

Let's go to the park.
공원에 나가자.

Go get your leash.
네 개줄을 가져와.

Do you wanna go for a run?
한번 달려 볼까?

Don't tug on the leash so hard!
줄을 그렇게 세게 당기지 마!

Slow down!
천천히 가!

Stay away from cars!
차에서 멀리 떨어져!

Come back here!
여기로 돌아와!

Who's that? Do you see a friend?
저 개는 누구야? 친구니?

Be nice to your friend.
친구한테 잘해 줘.

What do you smell?
무슨 냄새가 나니?

What are you sniffing?
뭘 그렇게 킁킁거리니?

Don't sniff there!
거기서 킁킁거리지 마!

Go see!
가서 확인해!

Let's play catch.
공놀이하자.

Go get it!
가서 집어 와!

Bring it here!
여기로 가져와!

Go fetch!
가서 가져와!

Drop it! (ball or stick)
내려 놔! (입에 물고 있는 공 또는 막대기)

Do you want to go for a swim?
수영하러 갈까?

You're a great swimmer.
수영 잘하는구나.

You're all wet!

흠뻑 젖었네!

Don't shake!

털지 마!

Let's go!

가자!

Time to go home now.

이제 집에 갈 시간이야.

10 Dirty Dog

목욕시키기

All dogs get dirty, and from time to time, they get too grubby and filthy to be inside the house. Below are a few phrases and expressions that may come in handy when speaking to a dirty dog.

모든 강아지들은 더러워진다. 때로는 너무나 더럽고 지저분해서 집 안으로 들이기가 어려운 경우도 발생한다. 더러워진 강아지를 다룰 때 유용하게 활용할 수 있는 표현을 몇 가지 소개한다.

You need a bath.
씻어야겠다.

It's your bath time.
목욕 시간이야.

Don't run away when I say bath time.
목욕하자고 할 때 도망가지 마.

What did you roll in?
어디에서 뒹굴었니?

What in the world did you get in to?
도대체 어디에 들어갔다 온 거니?

Did you get skunked?
스컹크한테 당하기라도 했어?

Look at you. You're a mess!
너 꼴 좀 봐라. 엉망이잖아!

Did you get sprayed by a skunk?
정말 지독한 냄새야. 스컹크한테 당하기라도 했니?

I need to get the tomato juice, baking soda and vinegar to get this smell out.
냄새를 없애려면 토마토 주스, 베이킹 소다, 식초가 필요하겠어.

I'm going to spray you with the garden hose.
너한테 호스로 물 좀 뿌려야겠다.

Get in the bathtub!
욕조 안으로 들어가!

You smell!
너한테 냄새가 나!

You smell like rotten fish.
네게서 썩은 생선 냄새가 나.

Where in the world have you been?
도대체 어디 갔다 온 거니?

How am I ever going to get you clean?
도대체 어떻게 너를 씻겨야 하니?

You are slobbering everywhere!
여기저기에다 침 흘리고 다니네!

Your eyes are leaking mucus, and it really smells!
눈곱이 끼어 냄새가 나!

Out!
나가!

Your paws are dirty!
발이 더럽잖아!

You are tracking mud all over the house!
온 집안에 흙을 묻혀 들이잖니!

You stepped in your own poo!
너 네 똥 밟았어!

You dirty dog!
이 더러운 강아지야!

You are smelly, wet, and dirty!
축축한 게 더럽잖아, 냄새도 나고 말이야!

Your breath smells!
네 입에서 냄새 나!

We need to brush your teeth.
네 이빨 좀 닦아야겠다.

You are shedding everywhere!
사방에 떨어진 네 털 좀 봐!

Your coat is oily.
털에 개기름이 좔좔 흐르네.

Your coat is filled with burrs.
털에 벼룩이 살림 차렸네.

You need to get brushed.
솔질 좀 해야겠어.

You look shaggy.
꾀죄죄하구나.

You need a haircut.
털 좀 깎아야겠다.

11 Car Rides

자동차 태우기

Most dogs love to ride in cars. Including your dog in special small trips to the store, or even long rides to the countryside, are additional ways to bond with your pet. Below are some basic conversational phrases to make even the smallest car trip to the store interesting.

대부분의 애완견은 자동차 타는 것을 좋아한다. 가게까지의 가까운 거리나 시골 여행에 애완견을 데리고 가는 것은 애완견과 친해질 수 있는 특별한 기회가 된다. 다음에 소개하는 간단한 표현들을 사용하면 쇼핑하러 가는 아주 가까운 거리라도 즐거워진다.

Do you want to go for a car ride?
자동차 탈래?

Let's go!
같이 가자!

Come on!
이리 와!

Get in!
타!

You can't drive!
너는 운전하면 안 돼!

Dogs don't drive!
개는 운전하는 거 아니야!

Get in the back seat!
뒷좌석에 타!

Sit still and stop moving around!
가만히 앉아 있어, 돌아다니지 말고!

I can't see!
안 보여!

Move over!
저리로 가!

Don't chew on that!
그것 물어뜯으면 안 돼!

Don't touch that!
그것 만지지 마!

Don't touch that button!
그 단추 건드리지 마!

You're excited, aren't you?
기분 좋구나?

Do you want to listen to the radio?
라디오 들을래?

Do you like this music?
이 음악 맘에 드니?

Stop howling out of tune!
음정도 틀리면서 그만 좀 흥얼거려!

You like to stick your head out the window, don't you?
창문 밖으로 머리를 내놓고 싶지?

Don't stick your head out!
창 밖으로 머리 내밀지 마!

Do you have to pee?
쉬해야겠어?

Do you have to poo?
똥 마려워?

Don't pee in the car!
차 안에서 쉬하면 안 돼!

Don't poo in the car!
차 안에서 똥 누지 마!

Do you feel sick?
아프니?

Please don't puke!
제발 토하지 말아 줘!

Oh no! You puked all over!
이런, 사방에 토해 놓았잖아!

Don't scratch the seat!
의자 좀 긁지 마!

You got hair all over the car!
차 안에 온통 네 털투성이야!

You'll go anywhere with me, won't you?
나랑 어디든지 갈 거지?

Don't slobber all over the car seat!
좌석에다 침 좀 흘리지 마!

Be good and don't bark!
얌전히 있어, 짖지 말고!

12 Dog Poops and Scoops

배설물 처리

Although it may not be pleasurable cleaning up after your dog, it is the law in most countries. In fact in NY City, before the enactment of a law that made it mandatory to clean up after your pet in 1978, approximately 40 million pounds of dog excrement were deposited on the streets each year. Below are a few phrases that are frequently used in such situations.

배설물 처리가 유쾌한 일은 아니지만, 대부분의 국가에서 애완견의 배설물을 처리하는 것을 법으로 정해놓고 있다. 사실 뉴욕시에서는 1978년 애완견 배설물 처리를 법으로 제정하기 전까지만 해도 매년 4천만 톤 정도의 배설물이 길거리에 방치되었었다. 애완견 배설물과 관련하여 자주 사용되는 몇 가지 표현을 소개한다.

Do you have to go?
똥 마렵니?

Are you telling me that you have to go?
똥 마렵다고 하는 거니?

What is that smell? Did you poo?
이게 무슨 냄새야? 너 똥 쌌니?

Don't pee on that!
거기다 쉬하지 마!

Don't poo over there!
거기다 똥 싸지 마!

Did you poo on this?
네가 여기에다 똥 쌌어?

Did you pee on this?
네가 여기에다 쉬했니?

Do you have to pee on every tree?
모든 나무에 네 쉬 냄새 풍겨야겠어?

I need to clean this mess up.
내가 네 똥 치워야 해.

Your poo is bigger than mine!
야, 네 똥 진짜 굵다!

I need to use the pooper-scooper.
배변 처리용 삽을 사용해야겠어.

Wait here until I clean this mess up.
네 똥 치울 때까지 여기서 기다려.

Don't step in your own poo!
네 똥 밟지 마!

What are you doing? Don't eat your own poo!
뭐 하는 거야? 네 똥 먹지 마!

This is disgusting!
이건 정말 구역질 나!

What did you eat?
너 뭐 먹었니?

We are going to have to change your diet.
네 먹이를 바꿔야겠어.

What a mess!
이게 뭐야, 더러워라!

You have to go on the newspaper.
신문지에다 똥 싸야지.

Your bathroom is here.
여기다 똥 싸는 거야.

Oh, this stinks!
이런, 이 냄새가 코를 찌르네!

13 Sleepy Dog

잠꾸러기 애완견

Dogs are asleep or drowsy more than half of the day and enjoy taking naps whenever. Many dogs are napping because of fatigue, but others do so simply out of boredom. Although rare, it is possible for dogs to have a sleeping disorder, nighttime anxiety, or even a fear of the dark due to failing eyesight. A night-light or some comforting words from his owner may be all your dog needs. Include your dog in as many activities as possible to let him know that he is important, too. Here are a few common conversational phrases that are used in such situations.

애완견들은 한나절 이상을 꾸벅꾸벅 졸고 있거나 늘 조는 상태이며 시도 때도 없이 낮잠을 즐기곤 한다. 피곤하기 때문에 낮잠을 자는 경우가 대부분이지만, 단지 따분하기 때문에 졸기도 한다. 아주 드물기는 하지만, 수면 장애나 야간 불안증 혹은 시력 저하로 인한 어둠에의 공포 때문인 경우도 있다. 스탠드를 켜 주거나 주인의 따뜻한 배려의 말 몇 마디가 애완견들이 바라는 전부인지도 모른다. 애완견을 가능한 많은 활동에 참여시킴으로써, 애완견이 스스로를 소중한 존재로 깨닫게 하자. 이러한 상황에서 유용하게 쓸 수 있는 표현을 몇 가지 소개한다.

Do you want to sleep up here on the bed with me?
침대로 올라와서 나랑 같이 잘까?

Are you cold?
추워?

Do you want me to turn the light on for you?
불 켜 줄까?

You make the bed nice and warm.
너 때문에 잠자리가 근사하고 따뜻하구나.

You can't sleep there. Get down!
거기서 자면 안 돼. 내려와!

Move over! That's my spot!
저리 가! 내 자리야!

Stop moving all over the bed! Pick one spot and stay there!
침대 여기저기로 돌아다니지 좀 마! 한 자리에 가만히 있으라고!

Stop hogging the bed!
침대에서 뛰지 마!

You slept all day.
하루 종일 자너라.

You must be tired.
피곤한가 보구나.

That's my chair!
그건 내 의자잖아!

Don't sleep on the couch!
소파 위에서 자면 안 돼!

Go to your own bed.
네 침대 가서 자.

You were whimpering in your sleep.
너 자면서 낑낑거리더라.

Were you chasing rabbits in your sleep?
꿈속에서 토끼 사냥이라도 했니?

Did you have a dream?
꿈 꿨어?

You slept like a bear.
깊이 자던걸.

You were snoring like a bear.
천둥처럼 코를 심하게 골던데.

You were snoring.
너 코 골면서 자더라.

Can you do anything else besides sleep?
자는 거 외에는 할 줄 아는 게 없니?

14 My Dog is Sick

아픈 애완견 돌보기

A key point to remember when speaking to an injured or sick dog is that they are sensitive animals. A soft and encouraging voice tone will be needed when handling any pet that doesn't feel well or is scared. A good way to calm your pet is to constantly tell him, "It's OK," while gently stroking the top of his head.

다쳤거나 아픈 애완견에게 말을 걸 때 명심해야 할 핵심 포인트는 그들이 예민한 동물이라는 점이다. 부드럽고 위로하는 목소리로 건강이 좋지 않거나 겁먹은 애완견들을 대할 필요가 있다. 애완견을 진정시키는 좋은 방법은 머리 윗부분을 부드럽게 쓰다듬으면서 "괜찮아"라고 계속 말해 주는 것이다.

Do you feel ok?
괜찮니?

You look sick!
아파 보이는구나!

What's the matter?
왜 그래?

Are you sick?
아프니?

You puked all over!
전부 토해 냈네!

Your nose is dry.
코가 말랐네.

I think that you have a cold.
감기 걸린 것 같은데.

Oh, you poor thing.
아, 가엾은 것.

You need some rest.
좀 쉬도록 하렴.

Does it hurt?
아프니?

Do you have a sore paw?
발이 쑤시니?

You have a thorn in your paw.
발에 가시가 박혔구나.

You're bleeding!
피가 나네!

This must hurt.
아프겠구나.

We should go to the vet.
동물 병원에 가야겠다.

What's wrong?
무슨 일이야?

It's time to get your shots.
주사 맞을 시간이네.

It's ok.
괜찮아.

You're so brave.
정말 용감하네.

Take this and you'll feel better.
약 먹어, 그럼 나아질 거야.

Time to take your medicine.
약 먹을 시간이다.

Don't run away when I say medicine.
약 먹자고 할 때 도망가지 좀 마.

Open your mouth!
입 벌려!

Swallow it!
삼켜!

Don't spit it out!
뱉어 내지 마!

Good boy!
잘했어!

Good girl!
잘했어!

Don't be afraid. Stop shaking!
겁내지 말고 그만 떨어!

You'll be ok.
괜찮아질 거야.

재주부리는 애완견

Dog tricks often begin as basic commands and then progress to more sophisticated taught behavior that is usually rewarded when done successfully. Dogs don't speak or understand any human language innately, so they have to be trained or taught. Refer to the section on "bonding" and "training your dog" before you attempt to teach your dog any tricks on your own. Below is a basic list of dog tricks.

재주부리기는 종종 명령의 기본 단계라 할 수 있다. 그 후 점차 세련된 훈련으로 진행되며, 잘한 행동에는 보통 포상이 따르게 마련이다. 애완견들은 선천적으로 인간의 언어를 이해하거나 말하지 못하기 때문에 훈련시키거나 길들여야 한다. 애완견에게 재주를 가르치려고 시도하기 전에 '애완견과 친해지기' 와 '훈련시키기' 부분을 참조하도록 한다. 다음은 재주부리기에 유용하게 쓸 수 있는 표현이다.

Roll over!
굴러!

Sit!
앉아!

Lay down!
엎드려! (누워!)

Stand up!
일어나!

Stay!
가만히 있어!

Come!
이리 와!

Heel!
바짝 따라와!

Jump!
뛰어올라!

Shake a paw.
악수.

The other one.
다른 손.

Play dead!
죽은 척해!

Speak!
짖어!

Go fetch!
가서 물어 와!

Good boy!
잘했어!

Good girl!
잘했어!

Do you want a treat?
상 줄까?

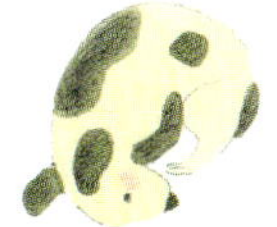

16 Dog Grooming

애완견 미용

Some owners take it upon themselves to groom their animals instead of leaving it to professionals. One may be able to understand a lot about a pet owner by how well the pet is groomed. For humans this may be a pleasurable experience, but in most cases for dogs, it is not. In fact, many dogs dread cleanliness and would much rather smell like your garbage. When grooming your pet, let him know that this is not punishment and that your pet will look and smell wonderful when you are done. Encourage him whenever possible. Remember not to be too strict with your pet when grooming.

어떤 주인들은 애완견 손질을 전문가에게 맡기기보다는 자신의 일이라고 여긴다. 애완견 손질 상태를 보고 주인에 대해 많은 것을 파악할 수 있을지도 모른다. 인간에게는 애완견을 손질하는 것이 즐거운 경험일 수도 있지만, 대부분의 강아지 경우에는 그렇지 못하다. 사실 많은 애완견들이 씻는 것을 두려워하여, 차라리 쓰레기 같은 악취를 풍기는 편이 낫다고 생각한다. 애완견을 손질할 때, 손질은 벌이 아니라 멋지게 하기 위한 것이며 좋은 향기를 풍기게 하려는 것이라는 점을 주지시킨다. 가능하면 자주 애완견을 격려하라. 강아지를 손질할 때는 너무 엄하게 다루지 않아야 한다는 점을 명심한다.

It's time for your haircut.
털 깎자.

Your hair is too long.
털이 너무 긴 것 같아.

I think that you are getting a little shaggy.
털북숭이가 되어 가는 것 같아.

Let's give you a summer haircut.
여름맞이 털깎기하자.

It is time to trim your coat.
털 좀 손질하자.

Don't move!
움직이지 마!

Don't be afraid of the dog clippers.
애견 미용사는 무서운 사람이 아니란다.

Don't run away when I get the dog clippers.
애견 미용사에게 가서 달아나면 안 돼.

Sit nice.
얌전히 있어.

Don't growl!
으르렁거리지 마!

I'll give you a treat if you sit still and be nice.
가만히 얌전하게 잘 있으면 상 줄게.

You have bad breath.
입냄새가 심한걸.

You need to get your teeth brushed.
너 이빨 좀 닦아야겠다.

We need to clean your ears. You have mites.
귀 청소 좀 해야겠다. 진드기가 있어.

You have a rotten tooth.
이가 하나 썩었네.

Don't be afraid!
무서워하지 마!

Time for your shampoo.
목욕하자.

Don't be afraid of the hair dryer.
헤어드라이어는 무서운 게 아니야.

You smell nice and clean.
말쑥하고 좋은 냄새가 나는구나.

You have a beautiful coat.
근사하게 잘랐네.

Do you want to dye your hair?
염색해 줄까?

You look great in pink.
분홍색이 잘 어울리는구나.

Your nails are too long.
발톱이 너무 긴걸.

Your nails need to be cut.
발톱 좀 잘라야겠다.

Do you want me to paint your nails?
발톱에 페디큐어 해줄까?

You look great!
멋진걸!

You look handsome!
잘생겼네!

You look pretty!
예쁘다!

You are the prettiest dog in town.
네가 우리 동네에서 제일 예뻐.

You are the most handsome dog in town.
네가 우리 동네에서 제일 잘생겼어.

Do you want a treat for sitting so nice?
얌전히 잘 있었으니까 상 줄까?

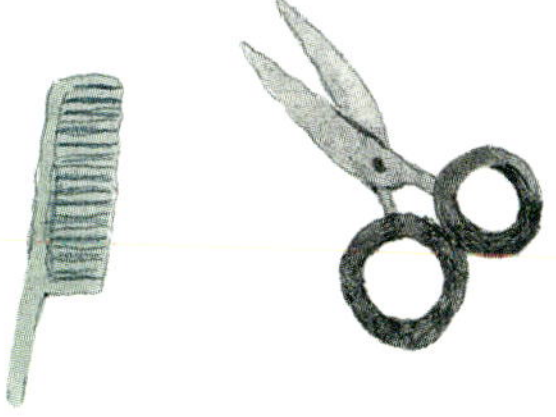

17 Good Dog

칭찬하기

Giving praise to your dog by smothering him with love and affection, and seeing him in high spirits for being praised, are probably the most rewarding moments of owning a pet. Below is a brief list of the more common phrases used when commending your canine companion.

사랑과 애정을 듬뿍 담아 애완견을 칭찬한 후 칭찬으로 인해 기가 산 애완견을 바라볼 때가 애견 주인으로서는 최고의 보람을 느끼는 순간일 것이다. 다음은 말벗인 애완견을 칭찬할 때 유용하게 사용할 수 있는 표현이다.

Good dog.
착한 것.

Good doggie.
착한 우리 아기.

You're a good dog, aren't you?
넌 착한 강아지야, 그렇지?

You're such a good dog, aren't you?
넌 정말 착한 강아지야, 그렇지?

You are my best friend.
넌 내 가장 친한 친구야.

You're the best dog in the whole world.
넌 세상에서 최고야.

You're so smart!
아주 영리하구나!

You're a genius!
넌 천재야!

That'a boy!
잘했어!

That'a girl!
잘했어!

You're the best!
넌 최고야!

You're a wonderful dog.
넌 굉장해.

You're awesome!
넌 아주 멋지구나!

You're such a sweetheart.
넌 사랑스러워.

You listen to everything I say.
내 말은 전부 귀담아듣네.

You are such a loyal friend.
넌 내 충직한 벗이란다.

I know that you love me.
네가 날 사랑한다는 걸 알아.

I love you too.
나도 널 사랑해.

Give me a kiss.
내게 입맞춰.

Come here and give me a hug.
이리 와, 어디 한번 안아 보자.

I love you more than I love the cat.
고양이보다 네가 더 좋아.

18 Bad Dog

야단치기

Although you may love your dog to pieces, there are times when he oversteps his limits and should be verbally punished for bad behavior. Remember to strengthen your voice tone and to abstain from physical punishment. Try to keep in mind that your dog does not behave badly, intentionally!

애완견을 아무리 사랑한다 할지라도, 애완견의 행동이 도를 넘어서게 되면 말로써 나쁜 행동을 꾸짖어야 할 경우가 있다. 목소리는 엄하게 하되 체벌은 삼가야 된다는 점을 명심한다. 애완견들이 의도적으로 나쁜 행동을 하는 것은 아니라는 사실도 잊지 말기를.

Bad dog!
못된 것!

Don't do that!
그러지 마!

You stupid dog!
멍청한 것!

You mutt!
이 똥개야!

Stop it!
그만!

No!
안 돼!

Spit that out!
뱉어!

You mangy mutt!
이 더러운 똥개야!

Stay out of there!
거기 들어가지 마!

Get out of there!
거기서 나와!

Get down!
내려가!

Stop barking!
그만 짖어!

Stop barking at the neighbor.
이웃 사람에게 짖지 마.

Stop howling, please.
제발 우는 소리 좀 내지 마.

Get out of the garbage!
쓰레기에서 썩 물러나!

Get off the couch!
소파에서 내려와!

I'm sending you to the dog pound!
너 개 수용소에 보내 버릴 테다!

Look at the mess you made!
네가 어질러 놓은 쓰레기 좀 봐!

Get over here!
이리 와!

Get!
나가! (가!)

Your hair is everywhere!
사방에 떨어진 네 털 좀 봐!

Don't chew on that!
그것 씹지 마!

Don't drink out of the toilet!
변기 물 먹지 마!

Don't chase the cat!
고양이 좀 내버려 둬!

Stop chasing the cat. You're going to give him a heart attack!
고양이 좀 쫓아다니지 마. 고양이가 심장마비 걸리겠다!

Don't scratch the walls!
벽을 긁지 마!

Get out of the garden!
정원에서 나오지 못해!

Don't chew on the furniture!
가구 좀 씹지 마!

Don't dig up the garden!
정원의 흙 좀 파내지 마!

Stop humping my leg!
내 다리에 비비지 좀 마!

What in the world were you thinking?
대체 무슨 생각으로 그런 거야?

Have you gone crazy?
너 미쳤어?

Look at What My Dog is Doing

애완견 관찰하기

Here are a few common phrases that you may wish to relate to a friend or another member of the family about your pet's behavior. Remember whatever your animal is doing, he thinks that it is a good idea, so don't rush to punish your pet for odd behavior.

다른 가족이나 친구에게 애완견의 행동에 대해 설명하고자 할 때 활용할 수 있는 몇 가지 표현을 소개한다. 명심할 점은, 애완견은 무엇을 하고 있든지 간에 스스로는 좋은 생각이라고 여기기 때문에 이상한 행동을 하더라도 성급하게 혼내서는 안 된다는 것이다.

My dog is watching the children.
우리 강아지는 아이들을 지켜보고 있어.

My dog is playing with the kids.
우리 강아지는 아이들과 놀아 주고 있어.

My dog is hiding from the vacuum.
우리 강아지는 청소기를 요리조리 피하는 중이야.

My dog is chasing his tail.
우리 강아지는 제 꼬리를 잡으려 하고 있어.

My dog is chasing the cat.
우리 강아지는 고양이를 쫓고 있어.

My dog is hiding, because he knows I am angry.
우리 강아지는 내가 화난 것을 알고서 숨었어.

My dog is chasing cars.
우리 강아지는 차를 쫓아다니고 있어.

My dog is drinking from the toilet.
우리 강아지는 변기 물을 먹고 있는 중이야.

My dog is humping my leg.
우리 강아지는 내 다리에 비비고 있어.

My dog is afraid of the cat.
우리 강아지는 고양이를 무서워해.

My dog is making me crazy.
우리 강아지 때문에 미치겠어.

My dog and cat are at war.
우리집 강아지와 고양이가 지금 전쟁 중이야.

My dog sleeps around.
우리 강아지는 바람둥이야.

My dog is sleeping.
우리 강아지는 자고 있어.

My dog is dreaming.
우리 강아지는 꿈속을 헤매는 중이지.

My dog is snoring.
우리 강아지는 코 골며 자고 있어.

My dog is whimpering.
우리 강아지는 처량하게 울고 있어.

My dog is sick.
우리 강아지는 지금 아파.

My dog is hurt.
우리 강아지는 다쳤어.

My dog is bleeding.
우리 강아지는 피가 나고 있어.

My dog's nose is dry.
우리 강아지는 코가 말랐어.

My dog is shaking.
우리 강아지는 몸을 털고 있어.

My dog is excited, because he knows that he is going outside.
우리 강아지는 밖으로 나갈 것을 알고 지금 흥분 상태야.

20 Look at What My Crazy Dog Did

애완견의 못 말리는 행동

During the course of owning a pet you may feel the need to explain certain behaviors or actions about your pet to other family members or friends. Below is a list of common phrases that may describe your pet's behavior. Remember, whatever your animal has done, he has a reason for it, so don't rush to punishment.

애완동물을 기르는 동안 다른 가족이나 친구들에게 애완동물에 관한 어떤 행동이나 활동을 설명할 필요성을 느끼게 될지도 모른다. 다음은 애완동물의 행동을 묘사하는 표현을 나열한 것이다. 명심할 점은 애완동물이 무슨 행동을 했든지 간에, 그 행동에 대한 이유가 나름대로 있기 때문에 성급하게 혼내려고 해서는 안 된다는 것이다.

My dog got pregnant again!
우리 강아지가 또 임신했어!

My dog did it!
우리 강아지가 그랬어!

My dog ran away!
도망가 버렸어!

My dog won't listen.
말을 들으려고 하지 않아.

My dog ate my son's Lego.
우리 아들의 레고 장난감을 삼켜 버렸어.

My dog got her ball stuck in my expensive leather shoes and chewed through the shoe to get it out.
우리 강아지가 내 비싼 가죽 구두에 자기 장난감 공을 집어넣고는 그걸 다시 꺼내려고 내 구두를 잘근잘근 씹어 놓은 것 있지.

My dog bit me!
나를 물었어!

My dog drooled all over the furniture.
가구 전체에다 침을 묻혀 놓았어.

My dog ripped a hole in my sweater.
내 스웨터를 물어뜯어 구멍을 내 놨어.

My dog tracked dirt all over the house.
온 집안에 더러운 발자국을 찍어 놨어.

My dog shed hair all over the house.
온 집안이 강아지 털투성이야.

My dog got into a fight.
우리 강아지가 싸움을 했어.

My dog chewed on our new furniture.
새로 들여 놓은 가구에 이빨 자국을 내 놨어.

My dog stepped in his own poo.
자기 똥을 밟았어.

My dog slobbered all over me.
내 온몸에 침을 묻혀 놓았어.

My dog peed on my friend's leg.
내 친구 다리에다 오줌을 쌌어.

My dog puked all over the couch.
소파에다 전부 토해 버렸어.

My dog needs to go to training school.
애견 훈련소로 보낼 필요가 있어.

My dog took the cat's toy and hid it.
고양이 장난감을 가져가서 숨겨 놓았어.

My dog keeps peeing in the same spot on the floor.
계속 거실의 같은 장소에 오줌을 싸고 있어.

My dog barked all night last night.
간밤에 밤새 짖어댔어.

My dog got hit by a car.
차에 치였어.

My dog always begs for food at the table.
우리 식사 중에 항상 먹을 걸 구걸한다니까.

My dog killed my neighbor's pet rabbit.
이웃집 애완 토끼를 물어 죽였어.

My dog ate all of my cat's food.
고양이 사료까지 전부 먹어 치워 버렸어.

21 At the Kennel

애견 위탁소

Although you may want to take your pet with you on every family vacation or business trip, there are times when it is just not possible and you need to take your dog to the kennel. If your pet has been to a kennel before, he probably remembers it and dreads going back. Dogs can suffer from separation anxiety, and this can lead to depression. Sending some of your pet's favorite toys, and perhaps a blanket, with him may make his stay a bit more bearable. Below are a few questions for you to ask the kennel master as well as some questions that the kennel master may have for you.

출장 가거나 휴가 때 애완견을 데려가고 싶을지라도 그것이 여의치 않아 할 수 없이 애완견을 위탁소에 맡겨야 할 경우가 있다. 만약 애완견이 이전에 위탁소에 맡겨진 경험이 있다면, 아마도 그것을 기억해 내고 다시 가기를 겁낼지도 모른다. 애완견은 불안감 때문에 고통을 받을 수 있으며 이는 우울증으로 발전될 수 있다. 좋아하는 장난감이나 담요를 딸려 보내면 참을 만할 수도 있다. 다음은 애완견 주인과 위탁소 주인 사이에 이루어질 수 있는 질문 내용이다.

What are your rates?
요금은 얼마인가요?

What time can I drop off my dog?
몇 시에 저희 강아지를 맡길 수 있나요?

What time can I come and get him?
몇 시에 다시 찾아갈 수 있나요?

Will you play with my dog or will you just let
him out?
저희 강아지랑 놀아 주시나요, 아니면 밖으로 내보내기만 하시나요?

How much exercise would my dog get each day?
매일 운동량은 어떻게 되나요?

Will you clean and bathe my dog?
저희 강아지를 손질하고 목욕시켜 주시나요?

How often do you clean the cages?
강아지 집은 얼마나 자주 청소하시나요?

What kind of food will you give my dog?
어떤 종류의 사료를 주시나요?

How often will you feed him?
사료를 얼마나 자주 주시나요?

Can I send some of my dog's toys with him?
저희 강아지 장난감들을 딸려 보내도 될까요?

Can I send my dog's bed with him?
저희 강아지 침대를 딸려 보내도 될까요?

What kind of beds do you have?
어떤 종류의 침대를 보유하고 계십니까?

How big are the sleeping quarters for my dog?
강아지 침실의 크기는 어떻게 되나요?

How many dogs will be staying with my dog?
몇 마리 정도의 강아지가 같이 지내게 되는 건가요?

How often do you check the dogs?
강아지 상태는 얼마나 자주 체크하시나요?

Will you call my dog's veterinarian if it is necessary?
필요하면 수의사를 부르시나요?

Do all of your dogs have vaccinations?
이곳에 온 강아지들은 모두 예방 접종이 된 상태인가요?

Do the dogs have contact with each other?
강아지들끼리 서로 접촉하게 되나요?

Kennel master
위탁소 주인이 묻는 말

How long will your dog be staying?
강아지를 얼마나 맡겨 두실 건가요?

What is your dog's name?
강아지 이름은 무엇인가요?

Is your dog male or female?
강아지가 암컷입니까, 수컷입니까?

What breed is your dog?
품종이 어떻게 되나요?

Has your dog been spayed?
난소를 제거했나요?

Has your dog been neutered?
거세 수술을 했나요?

Has your dog been vaccinated?
예방 접종은 하셨나요?

How is your dog with other dogs?
다른 강아지들과 잘 지내나요?

Does your dog have any health problems?
건강상의 다른 문제는 없나요?

When will you be picking up your dog?
언제 강아지를 데려가실 건가요?

Do you have a special diet for your dog?
따로 먹이시는 강아지 사료가 있나요?

Has your dog ever bitten anyone?
사람을 문 적이 있나요?

22 Goodbyes

작별 인사

Saying goodbye to a pet, even for a short period of time, may not be as hard as saying goodbye to a spouse or loved one but it certainly is not easy. Leaving your pet can be quite difficult for him as well. Here are a few basic phrases for those sad goodbyes.

단기간일지라도 애완동물에게 작별 인사를 하는 것은, 배우자나 사랑하는 사람에게 작별 인사를 하는 것 만큼은 힘들지 않겠지만 결코 쉬운 일은 아니다. 작별은 애완견에게도 힘든 일일 수도 있다. 슬픈 작별 인사에 대한 몇 가지 기본적인 표현을 소개한다.

88

Goodbye.
잘 있어.

I'll be back again soon.
빨리 돌아올게.

Jay and Christa will take good care of you until
I get back.
내가 돌아올 때까지 제이랑 크리스타가 잘 돌봐 줄 거야.

Be a good dog while I am gone.
나 없는 동안 착하게 굴어야 해.

I'll miss you.
보고 싶을 거야.

This is your new home.
여기가 네 새집이란다.

I love you.
사랑한다.

Please don't forget about me.
날 잊지 말아줘.

I will never forget you.
널 절대 잊지 않을 거야.

I am sorry to say goodbye.
헤어지게 돼서 유감이구나.

You'll be happy here.
여기서도 행복할 거야.

You are the best dog that I ever had.
넌 내가 기른 강아지 중 최고야.

You are the best friend that I ever had.
넌 내게 있어 가장 좋은 친구야.

If we meet in another life, I'll be your dog, and
you can be my master.
다음 세상에서는 난 네 강아지로 넌 내 주인으로 다시 만나자꾸나.

Training your dog can be a most rewarding experience. It helps you understand the animal that you live with, and it creates a bond of loyalty. The more time that you invest in training your dog, the more he will understand you. The more you play with your dog, the more you will understand him.

강아지를 훈련시키는 것은 가장 보람 있는 일이 될 수 있다. 왜냐하면 강아지 훈련을 통하여 함께 살고 있는 강아지를 이해할 수 있고 강아지의 충성심을 유도할 수 있기 때문이다. 강아지 훈련에 많은 시간을 투자하면 할수록 강아지는 당신을 더 잘 이해할 수 있게 된다. 또한 강아지와 많은 시간을 놀아 줄수록 강아지를 더 잘 이해할 수 있게 될 것이다.

Train Your Dog

애완견 훈련시키기

23 Bonding with Your Dog

애완견과 친해지기

Creating a loving and caring relationship with your dog is the key to building trust and loyalty. Before you begin training your dog, you must first bond with your pet by establishing a mutual trusting relationship that grows with time. When your animal feels comfortable and [1]secure in his position as a new family member, he will respond favorably when trained. The concept of bonding with your animal is quite simple. Love your dog, and he will love you back. If you have had a dog for a while and want to change the way your relationship is going, this can be done as well. All you need to do is change the way you treat your pet.

애완견과 애정 어린 관계를 만드는 것은 신뢰와 충성을 싹트게 하는 열쇠이다. 애완견을 훈련 시키기에 앞서, 시간을 두고 신뢰 관계를 구축하여 결속을 다져야 한다. 애완견이 새로운 가족의 일원이 되어 편안함과 안정감을 느낄 때 비로소 훈련에 긍정적으로 반응하기 때문이다. 애완견과 친해진다는 개념은 간단하다. 즉 자신의 강아지를 사랑하면 강아지도 주인을 사랑하게 될 것이다. 이미 애완견을 기르고 있는데 애완견과의 관계를 바꾸고 싶다면 이 또한 얼마든지 가능하다. 그저 강아지를 대하는 방법을 바꾸면 된다.

How to begin...

If you have a young newborn pet, it is quite easy to
begin bonding as you are the first to take care of and
treat the animal. However, if you have received an older
pet, it may be a little more difficult to begin the bond,
since you may not know how well the dog was treated
by his previous owner. Regardless of the circumstances,
you must, immediately and consistently, let your dog
know that he is safe, loved, and respected. Let your dog
explore his new home and get to know each and every
member of the family freely, forgiving any accidents that
may occur. He should receive a lot of [2]affection from
everyone. Hug him, play with him, and by all means,
talk to him. Even though he doesn't understand what
you are saying, he will feel affection through the tone of
your voice.

시작하기

만약 막 태어난 새끼 강아지라면 당신이 강아지를 맨 처음 돌보는 사람이므로 강아지와 친해지
기가 쉽다. 그러나 조금 성장한 강아지라면 이전 주인이 그 강아지를 어떻게 다뤘는지를 알 수
없기 때문에 친해지기가 그리 쉽지는 않을 것이다. 상황이야 어떻든 강아지가 안전하며 사랑과
존중을 받고 있다는 느낌을 받을 수 있도록 신속히 그리고 일관되게 주지시켜야 할 것이다. 강
아지가 새로운 보금자리를 구석구석 살피고 가족 모두를 자유롭게 탐색할 수 있는 기회를 충분
히 주며, 그 와중에 실수를 하더라도 용서해 준다. 강아지는 모든 사람으로부터 사랑을 듬뿍 받
아야 한다. 강아지를 껴안고 같이 놀아 주며 다정하게 말을 건넨다. 강아지가 비록 당신의 밀을
알아듣지 못한다고 해도, 당신의 목소리 톤에서 사랑 받고 있음을 느낄 수 있을 것이다.

Bonding

There will never be a time when your pet is suddenly
bonded and feels safe. Bonding is a slow process of
enjoying and loving your animal while including him in
your daily activities. Below are 9 activities that promote

bonding between you and your dog. Keep in mind that
bonding is a gradual process that takes time and does
not happen overnight.

친해지기

강아지가 금세 편안함을 느끼고 당신과 친해질 수는 없을 것이다. 강아지를 사랑하고 즐거운 시
간을 함께 보낼 때, 그리고 일상 생활을 강아지와 함께할 때 비로소 강아지와 친해질 수 있다.
애완견과 친해질 수 있는 효과적인 9가지 방법을 소개하고자 한다. 강아지와 친해지기 위해서
는 시간이 필요하며, 하루아침에 되는 일이 아님을 명심해야 할 것이다.

1. Feeding Your Dog

When feeding your dog, be sure that you are speaking
in a [3]pleasurable tone, and be gentle when handling his
food dishes, even if you are just giving him
leftovers.

먹이기

강아지에게 먹이를 줄 때, 상냥한 목소리로 말한다. 비록 남은 음
식을 줄지라도 개밥그릇을 부드럽게 다루도록 한다.

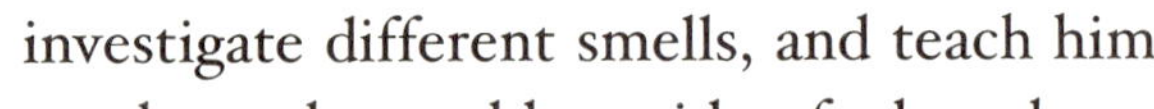

2. Walking Your Dog

Walking your dog is a special way to bond with your
[4]canine companion, because it is not a necessity like
feeding. This is a special time that you are investing in
your relationship with your pet. Be sure to allow him to
investigate different smells, and teach him
about the world outside of where he
lives. Even if he doesn't understand a
word that you are saying, he will
know that you are trying, and that
you love him.

애완견을 산책시키는 것은 먹이를 주는 것처럼 필수적인 활동은 아니기 때문에 애완견과 친해질 수 있는 특별한 방법이라고 말할 수 있다. 산책은 애완견과 친해지기 위해 투자하는 특별한 시간이다. 강아지가 산책 중에 여러 가지 다른 냄새를 맡아 볼 수 있도록 허용하고 집 밖의 세상에 대해서 배울 수 있도록 배려한다. 비록 애완견이 당신이 말하는 것을 알아듣지 못하더라도 당신의 노력과 사랑은 느낄 수 있을 것이다.

3. Bathing Your Dog

Like feeding, bathing your dog is a necessity, so the manner of which it is performed is important. Keep in mind that your dog would prefer smelling more like garbage than roses as it is a natural instinct for him. When bathing your animal, don't be too firm or strict. Don't be rough! Be sure to be extra careful when cleaning around your dog's sensitive ears. You should always speak cheerfully, and smother your animal with love, even when you are doing something you both dislike.

목욕시키기

먹이주기와 같이 애완견을 목욕시키는 일은 필수적인 활동이며, 어떻게 시키느냐가 중요하다. 강아지는 본능적으로 장미꽃 같은 좋은 냄새보다는 쓰레기 같은 고약한 냄새를 더 좋아한다는 점을 기억하라. 강아지를 목욕시킬 때 너무 엄격하게 다루지 않는다. 부드럽게 대하라. 특히 예민한 부위인 귀 부분을 목욕시킬 때에는 조심해서 다루도록 한다. 당신과 강아지 모두에게 싫은 일이라 할지라도 상냥하게 말하고 사랑을 듬뿍 주도록 한다.

4. Taking Your Dog Out

Whether you know it or not, your dog has emotions, and one of them is [5]boredom. Taking your dog out of the house, which he watches around the clock, on a special trip is a good way to bond with your pet. Be

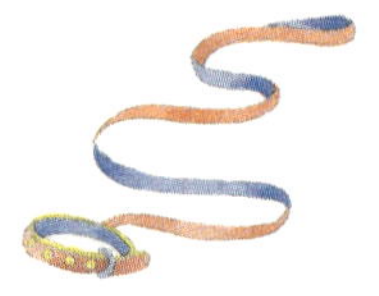

sure to tell your pet that you are going for a ride, and try arousing excitement in him before you go.

함께 외출하기

당신이 알든 알지 못하든 간에, 강아지도 감정이 있으며 그 중 하나가 무료함이다. 하루종일 지키고 있는 집을 떠나 특별한 여행을 떠나는 것은 강아지와 친해질 수 있는 좋은 방법이다. 여행을 떠나기 전, 강아지에게 차를 타고 여행을 떠날 것이라는 말을 해서 신바람나게 만든다.

5. Doing Chores with Your Dog

Although your dog probably can't help much with household chores, talking to him while you clean up, or do the laundry, will help your animal feel accepted in the family. The feeling of being accepted is essential for the bonding process.

집안일 같이 하기

비록 강아지가 별도움이 되지 않더라도, 집안 청소나 빨래를 할 때 강아지에게 말을 건넨다. 그렇게 함으로써, 강아지는 가족의 일원이라는 느낌을 받을 수 있다. 가족의 일원이라는 느낌은 강아지와 친해지는 과정에서 꼭 필요한 것이다.

6. Playing with Your Dog

Playing with your dog is also especially important for bonding, because, while playing, there is a lot of time for contact and dialogue between dog and owner. Your dog will appreciate the time that you spend with him.

놀아 주기

강아지와 놀아 주는 것은 친해지기 위해 반드시 필요한 것이다. 왜냐하면, 노는 과정에서 강아지와 주인 사이에 신체적 접촉과 대화가 자연스럽게 이루어지기 때문이다. 강아지는 당신과 함께 보내는 시간을 고맙게 생각할 것이다.

7. Exercising with Your Dog

Playing with your dog is not enough. You need to exercise him by taking him for walks or runs. Try to have a daily routine in which you exercise at about the same time each day. This is not only stress relieving for both you and your pet but, also, a foundation for bonding.

운동시키기

강아지와 놀아 주는 것만으로는 부족하다. 산책을 하거나 같이 달리면서 운동을 시킨다. 매일 같은 시간대에 운동시키는 것이 바람직하다. 강아지를 운동시키면 서로의 스트레스가 풀리는 것은 물론 친해질 수 있는 토대가 형성된다.

8. Housebreaking or Paper Training

Training your pet to be [6]housebroken is also a bonding experience. Although you may not know it, your pet wants to please you by doing what you want. When your pet has become housebroken, and sees that good learning behavior has rewards, he will try to please you more often.

배변 훈련

배변 훈련도 또한 강아지와 친해지는 효과적인 경험이다. 잘 모를 수도 있겠지만, 애완견은 주인이 원하는 것을 행함으로써 주인을 기쁘게 해주고 싶어한다. 강아지가 오줌, 똥을 제대로 가리게 되고 잘한 행동에는 보상이 따른다는 사실을 깨닫게 되면, 더욱 자주 당신을 기쁘게 하려고 노력할 것이다.

9. Consistent Daily Routines

Everyday consistent daily routines such as feeding, walking, and playing with your dog will foster good bonding between you and your pet. Be sure that you are not feeding your dog when he barks or asks for food. Make it a daily routine to feed him at exact times during the day. Your dog will realize that he is included in his master's activities, and he will try much harder to please you.

정해진 시간에 일상 활동 실시하기
매일 강아지에게 먹이를 주고 산책시키고 놀아 주면 강아지와 친해질 수 있다. 강아지가 짖거나 음식을 달라고 요구할 때 먹이를 주지 말고, 매일 정확한 시간에 먹이를 주도록 한다. 그렇게 하면, 강아지는 자신이 주인의 일상 활동의 일부라는 점을 깨닫고 주인을 기쁘게 하기 위해 더욱 노력할 것이다.

1 secure 안전한　**2 affection** 애정　**3 pleasurable** 〈사물이〉즐거운, 만족한
4 canine 개의　**5 boredom** 권태　**6 housebroken** 집안에서 길들인, 배변 훈련이 된 = paper-trained

24 Training Your Dog

훈련시키기

Training your dog can be a most rewarding experience. It helps you understand the animal that you live with, and it creates a bond of loyalty. The more time that you invest in training your dog, the more he will understand you. The more you play with your dog, the more you will understand him.

My neighbors have two Korean purebred Jindo dogs who have a rather wild behavior. I approached the owners and spoke to them about the manner in which they trained their dogs but they told me that they hadn't trained their purebreds. They preferred to let them live as their ancestors did—wild!

In the past, every dog had a specific purpose, whether it was to guard sheep, guide cattle, or find lost or buried skiers. Domesticated dogs can quickly become bored and depressed when neglected. [1]Neglect may lead to improper behavior like over barking, chewing on furniture, and even aggressive [2]tendencies toward others. These are all stress related behaviors stemming from poor training.

Just loving your dog is not enough. All dogs need a certain amount of training to fully become loyal loving pets and companions, although some need more than others.

If dogs are man's best friend, then we should treat our friends with the same respect and love that they are able to treat us with. Below are 5 basic tricks to teach your pet. Before trying some of the harder tricks, these fundamental 5 tricks may be the most [3]appropriate.

1 neglect 무관심, 방치   **2 tendency** 성향   **3 appropriate** 적합한

강아지를 훈련시키는 것은 가장 보람 있는 일이 될 수 있다. 왜냐하면 강아지 훈련을 통하여 함께 살고 있는 강아지를 이해할 수 있고 강아지의 충성심을 유도할 수 있기 때문이다. 강아지 훈련에 많은 시간을 투자하면 할수록 강아지는 당신을 더 잘 이해할 수 있게 된다. 또한 강아지와 많은 시간을 놀아 줄수록 강아지를 더 잘 이해할 수 있게 될 것이다.

이웃 중에 두 마리의 순종 진돗개를 키우는 사람이 있는데, 그 진돗개들은 상당히 사납다. 나는 그 이웃에게 가서 개를 훈련시키는 방법에 대해 얘기했다. 하지만 그들은 훈련시키지 않고 진돗개의 본성대로 살게 하겠다고 말했다. 사납게 말이다!

과거에는 모든 개들에게는 특별한 목적이 있었다. 어떤 개는 양과 가축을 지키는 용도로 쓰였고 어떤 개는 스키를 타다 길을 잃거나 눈에 파묻혀 버린 사람들을 구조할 목적으로 쓰였다. 애완견들은 방치되면 쉽게 지루해 하거나 우울해 한다. 방치는 지나치게 짖는다든지, 가구를 물어뜯든지, 심지어 사람들에게 공격적인 성향을 보이는 비정상적인 행동으로 이어진다. 이 증상들은 모두 부적절한 훈련에서 야기되는 스트레스에서 나오는 것이다.

강아지를 사랑하는 것만으로는 충분치 않다. 모든 강아지들이 충직하고 사랑스런 애완견이자 동반자가 되기 위해서는 어느 정도의 훈련이 필요하다. 물론 애완견의 종류에 따라 훈련의 강도는 달라질 수 있지만 말이다.

만약 강아지가 인간의 가장 좋은 친구라면 강아지들이 인간에게 보여 주는 사랑과 존경에 걸맞도록 강아지들을 대해야 할 것이다. 지금부터 5가지 강아지 훈련법을 소개하고자 한다. 좀더 어려운 훈련을 시키기 전에 이 5가지 기본 훈련법이 가장 적당할 것이다.

25 Teaching Your Dog to Sit

1. Go to a quiet place away from distractions.
   방해받지 않는 조용한 장소로 간다.

2. Be ready with a small piece of your dog's favorite treat.
   강아지가 좋아하는 것을 상으로 준비한다.

3. Stand facing your dog or puppy. Holding the treat in front of your dog's nose, move the treat up toward the top of his head, high enough that he can just barely reach it.
   강아지와 마주 선다. 강아지 코앞에 강아지가 좋아하는 것을 두었다가 강아지 머리 위로 들어 올린다. 이때, 강아지가 서 있는 상태에서 겨우 잡을 수 있을 정도의 높이까지만 상을 들어 올린다.

4. If your dog lifts his front feet off the ground, you are holding the treat too high. When your dog lifts his head and shoulders to get the treat, his bottom should go down.
   만약 강아지가 앞발을 들어야 잡을 수 있다면, 너무 높이 들어올린 것이다. 상을 잡으려고 머리와 어깨를 들어올리지만, 엉덩이는 바닥에 닿도록 한다.

5. As soon as your dog is in the sit position, praise him by saying, "Sit! Good boy, sit!" Hug him and give him a treat.
   강아지가 앉자마자 "앉아! 잘했어, 앉아!"라고 칭찬해 준다. 강아지를 껴안고 상을 준다.

6. If you need to, gently touch your dog's back, giving him a signal that you want him to sit.

필요하다면 강아지의 등을 살짝 건드린다. 강아지를 앉히려면 강아지의 등을 건드려서 신호를 보낸다.

7. Never punish your dog if he doesn't sit when told to. He is just learning, and scaring your dog will just confuse him even more.

앉으라고 했는데 듣지 않았다고 해서 벌을 주지 않는다. 강아지는 지금 배우고 있는 중이며, 강아지를 두렵게 하면 혼란만 가중시킬 뿐이다.

8. When you give the command to sit, say it only once. Don't repeat it, because your dog will learn that he doesn't have to sit the very first time he hears the command.

앉으라는 명령은 한 번만 한다. 명령을 반복해서 말하지 않도록 한다. 반복해서 말하게 되면 강아지는 처음 명령을 들었을 때 곧바로 하지 않아도 된다고 생각할 수 있기 때문이다.

It may take 10 times before your dog understands what is happening. When you think he knows the word "sit," try it without the treat. If he doesn't sit, don't say anything. Just try it with a treat again. Praise him and smother him with affection whenever he does what he is supposed to do.

훈련 내용을 익히는 데는 10번 정도의 반복 연습이 필요할 것이다. '앉아'에 익숙해졌다고 생각되면 상을 주는 것 없이 연습시켜 본다. 만약 강아지가 앉지 않으면 아무 말도 하지 않는다. 상을 이용하여 다시 시도해 본다. 강아지가 말을 잘 들으면 칭찬하고 사랑을 듬뿍 준다.

26 Teaching Your Dog to Stay

1. Go to a quiet place away from distractions.
   방해받지 않는 조용한 장소로 간다.

2. Be ready with a small piece of your dog's favorite treat.
   강아지가 좋아하는 것을 상으로 준비한다.

3. Have your dog sit, making sure he is sitting comfortably.
   강아지를 앉게 한다. 편안하게 앉아 있는지 확인한다.

4. Stand to his right, put the palm of your hand in front of his face, and say, "Stay!"
   강아지의 오른쪽에 선 후, 손바닥을 강아지의 얼굴 앞에다 대고 "가만히 있어!"라고 말한다.

5. Step away using your right foot. You should always leave your dog using your right foot.
   오른발부터 떼면서 걸어 나간다. 강아지에게서 멀어질 때는 반드시 오른발부터 뗀다.

6. Take only one or two steps, turn, and stand right in front of your dog.
   1~2 발자국을 옮긴 후, 다시 돌아와 강아지의 오른쪽에 선다.

7. Wait a few seconds, and return to your dog's side.
   잠깐 기다렸다가 강아지 옆으로 돌아간다.

8. When you finish, say, "Okay!" Get your dog to move, and give him a big hug and a kiss. Really praise him!

끝나고 난 후, "잘했어!"라고 말한다. 이제 강아지가 움직이도록 허락하고 꼭 껴안고 뽀뽀 해 준다. 진심에서 우러나오는 칭찬을 한다.

9. Do this several times over the next few days. When your dog seems steady, you can increase the time that you stand in front of him.

며칠간 이 훈련을 몇 번 반복한다. 강아지가 잘하면 강아지 앞에 서 있는 시간을 늘린다.

10. Increase the distance, but only a little at a time.

거리도 늘려 본다. 그러나 한 번에 조금씩만 늘린다.

11. Practice your "stays" from a down or standing position by following the same steps.

강아지가 앉거나 서 있는 상태에서 기다리는 연습을 시킬 때도 같은 방식을 활용한다.

12. If you want to give your dog a treat, give him small pieces while he's in the "stay" position. Don't feed him after he moves, or he will have trouble staying while he is waiting for the treat.

강아지에게 상을 주고 싶으면, 강아지가 가만히 있는 상태에서 상을 준다. 강아지가 움직 이고 난 후에는 상을 주지 않는다. 그렇게 하지 않으면 상을 기다리느라 가만히 있지 못 할 것이다.

13. Never punish your dog if he doesn't sit when told to. He is just learning, and scaring your dog will just confuse him even more.

가만히 있으라고 말했는데 움직였다고 해서 벌을 내리지 않는다. 강아지는 지금 배우고 있 는 중이며, 강아지를 두렵게 하면 혼란만 가중시킬 뿐이다.

14. When you give the command to stay, say it only once. Don't repeat it, because your dog will learn that he doesn't have to stay the very first time he hears the command.

'가만히 있어'라는 명령은 한 번만 한다. 명령을 반복해서 말하지 않는다. 반복해서 말하 면 강아지는 처음 명령을 들었을 때 곧바로 하지 않아도 된다고 생각할 수 있기 때문이다.

It may take 10 times before your dog understands what is happening. When you think he knows the word "stay," try it without the treat. If he doesn't stay, don't say anything. Just try it with a treat again. Praise him and smother him with affection whenever he does what he is supposed to do.

훈련 내용을 익히는 데는 10번 정도의 반복 연습이 필요할 것이다. '가만히 있어'라는 명령에 익숙해졌다고 생각되면 상 주는 것 없이 연습시켜 본다. 만약 강아지가 가만히 있지 않으면, 아무 말도 하지 않는다. 상을 이용하여 한번 시도해본다. 강아지가 말을 잘 들으면 칭찬하고 사랑을 듬뿍 준다.

27 Teaching Your Dog to Come

"이리 와!"

1. Go to a quiet place away from distractions.
   방해받지 않는 조용한 장소로 간다.

2. Be ready with a small piece of your dog's favorite treat.
   강아지가 좋아하는 것을 상으로 준비한다.

3. Put a leash on your dog.
   강아지 목에 줄을 건다.

4. Have treats in your pocket, if you like.
   원한다면 강아지에게 줄 상을 준비해 넣어 간다.

5. With your dog on your left side, start walking. Take 5 or 6 steps. Don't worry if your dog is pulling on the leash.
   강아지를 당신의 왼쪽에 두고 걷기 시작한다. 5~6발자국을 뗀다. 강아지가 줄을 잡아당겨도 걱정할 필요는 없다.

6. When you are ready, stop, back up, and call your dog to you, coaxing him with the leash gently.
   준비가 되면, 멈춰 서서 몇 발짝 뒤로 간 후 강아지를 부른다. 이때 개줄을 가볍게 당긴다.

7. When he gets to you, smother him with praise and give him a treat.
   강아지가 당신에게 오면, 칭찬하면서 상을 준다.

8. Never punish your dog if he doesn't get to you when told to. He is just learning, and scaring your dog will just confuse him even more.

명령을 들었는데도 따르지 않는다고 해서 벌을 주지는 않는다. 강아지는 지금 배우고 있는 중이며, 강아지를 두렵게 하면 혼란만 가중시킬 뿐이다.

9. When you give the command to "come," say it only once. Don't repeat it, because your dog will learn that he doesn't have to come the very first time he hears the command.

'이리 와'라는 명령은 한 번만 한다. 명령을 반복해서 말하지 않는다. 반복해서 말하면 강아지가 처음 명령을 들었을 때 곧바로 하지 않아도 된다고 생각할 수 있기 때문이다.

10. Repeat 2-3 times each day.

매일 2~3회 반복한다.

Note

It may take 10 times before your dog understands what is happening. When you think he knows the word "come," try it without the leash or treat. If he doesn't come, don't say anything. Just try it with the leash and the treat again. Praise him and smother him with affection whenever he does what he is supposed to do.

훈련 내용을 익히는 데는 10회 정도의 반복 연습이 필요할 것이다. '이리 와'에 익숙해졌다고 생각되면 개줄이나 상 없이 연습시켜 본다. 만약 강아지가 오지 않으면, 아무런 말도 하지 않는다. 상을 이용하여 다시 시도해 본다. 강아지가 말을 잘 들으면 칭찬하고 사랑을 듬뿍 준다.

"악수!"

1. Be ready with a small piece of your dog's favorite treat.
   강아지가 좋아하는 것을 상으로 준비한다.

2. Tell your dog, "Sit!" (Place your hand on his back and gently push down if needed.)
   강아지에게 "앉아!"라고 말한다. (필요하면 등에 손을 얹고 살짝 눌러 준다.)

3. Crouch down in front of your dog, extend your right hand, and say, "Shake a paw!"
   강아지 앞에 웅크리고 앉아 오른손을 내밀고 "악수!"라고 말한다.

4. If your dog licks your hand or stands up, tell your dog to sit and stay before trying again. This time, if your dog still doesn't respond correctly, you should reach out further, grasp his paw, and repeat the command, "Shake a paw!" while moving your dog's paw up and down as if you were shaking hands with him.
   만약 강아지가 당신의 손을 핥거나 일어서려고 하면, 다시 새로 시도하기에 앞서 앉아서 가만히 있으라고 말한다. 강아지가 제대로 반응을 보이지 않으면 당신의 팔을 더 뻗어 강아지의 앞발을 잡고 "악수!"라고 명령한다. 이때 강아지의 앞발을 잡고 마치 악수를 하듯이 위아래로 흔든다.

5. Immediately after you have shaken your dog's paw, you should reward your dog with praise and smother

him with affection.
강아지의 앞발을 흔들자마자 강아지를 칭찬하고 사랑을 듬뿍 준다.

6. Practice this several times daily for several days.
머칠 동안 매일 수 차례 반복한다.

7. If your dog learns this trick, you can try having him shake the other paw by changing hands and saying, "Shake the other one!" Be sure that your dog sees you change hands.
강아지가 이 훈련에 익숙해지면, 당신의 손을 바꾸면서 "다른 손 악수!"라고 말하고, 다른 손을 내미는 훈련을 시킨다. 강아지로 하여금 당신이 손을 바꾸는 행동을 확실히 보게 한다.

Note

It may take 5 times or so before your dog understands what is happening. When you think he knows the command, "Shake a paw!" try teaching him to shake the other paw. If he doesn't shake a paw, don't correct him harshly. Praise him and smother him with affection whenever he does what he is supposed to do.

훈련 내용을 익히는 데는 5회 정도의 반복 연습이 필요할 것이다. "악수!"라는 명령에 익숙해졌다고 생각하면 다른 발도 연습시킨다. 만약 강아지가 발을 내밀지 않더라도 심하게 대하지 않는다. 말을 잘 들었을 때에는 칭찬하고 사랑을 듬뿍 주도록 한다.

29 Teaching Your Dog to Lie Down

"엎드려!"

1. Have your dog sit or stand. Let your dog sniff the treat you are holding, but don't let him have it.

    강아지를 앉거나 서도록 한다. 당신이 상으로 들고 있는 것을 강아지가 냄새 맡는 것은 허용하되 주지는 않는다.

2. Lower the treat to the floor, and as you are doing that, your dog should follow it down.

    상을 바닥 쪽으로 내린다. 당신이 그렇게 하면 강아지도 따라서 몸을 낮출 것이다.

3. Be sure to say, "Lie down!" as your dog begins to lower himself.

    강아지가 몸을 낮출 때, "엎드려!"라고 말한다.

4. Your dog should lower himself all the way to the floor.

    강아지가 바닥까지 납작 엎드리도록 한다.

5. Only give him the treat once he is on the floor. Don't repeat, "Lie down!" many times. Say, "Good boy, lie down!" instead.

    강아지가 바닥에 납작 엎드렸을 때만 상을 주도록 한다. "엎드려!"라는 말을 반복하지 않는다. 대신 "착하지, 엎드려!"라고 말한다.

6. Practice this several times during the day and over several days.

    며칠 동안 매일 수 차례 훈련을 반복한다.

After your dog has learned the command "Lie down!" you can practice it with "stay." It's okay to let your dog lie down and stay for 15 or 20 minutes, and it's okay if he falls asleep. Once in a while, it is helpful when he needs to calm down.

강아지가 '엎드려!' 라는 명령을 익힌 후에는 '가만히 있어' 라는 명령어와 함께 연습해 본다. 강아지를 엎드리게 하여 15분이나 20분 동안 가만히 있게 할 수도 있다. 훈련 도중 잠이 들어도 무방하다. 강아지가 흥분을 가라앉힐 필요가 있을 때 유용한 명령어이다.

Dogs seem to have the amazing ability to sense what we cannot, and to communicate to us in ways that we don't understand. Dogs are absolutely unselfish friends of man, acting as protectors and inspirations to many.

The following are the author's personal collection of ten true short stories for dog-lovers, featuring incredible canines and their heartwarming loyalty to man.

개는 인간은 감지하지 못하는 것을 감지할 수 있는 놀라운 능력을 가지고 있는 것 같다. 또한 우리가 이해하지 못하는 방식으로 우리와 소통하는 것으로 생각된다. 개는 정말로 인간의 이기적이지 않은 친구로, 많은 사람들에게 보호자이자 감화를 주는 동물이다.

다음은 필자가 애견가들을 위해 모은 실화이다. 놀라운 애완견들을 주인공으로 하는 열 편의 짤막한 이야기는 인간에 대한 그들의 따뜻한 충성심을 보여준다.

3

Amazing but True Dog Stories

놀라운 애완견 이야기

30 Nasser the Wonder Dog

명견 나세르

It was one of the hottest summers on record. The trees surrounding Steve Smith's property did not display their normal [1]lushness, because it had not rained for months. In spite of the heat, Steve's neighbor jogged with his two black labs every day. Like Steve's neighbor John, the two black labs were friendly and, from time to time, would stop and play with Nasser, Steve's [2]mastiff.

One day, when Mr. Smith was in the kitchen, he heard Nasser bark [3]frantically at the front door. When he opened it, Nasser ran to meet the two black labs that were in the front yard. The three of them [4]galloped up the road barking feverously at John, who had collapsed on the road and was not displaying any signs of life. Another neighbor, who heard the [5]commotion and looked to see what was happening, called an ambulance.

Heat exhaustion was the cause of the collapse, and John did recover. All three dogs displayed a loyalty and caring that made Steve and John very proud.

---

1 lushness 푸르게 우거짐, 싱싱함   **2 mastiff** 큰 맹견의 일종   **3 frantically** 미친 듯이
4 gallop 질주하다   **5 commotion** 소동, 야단

1. What was the weather like?
어떤 날씨였나?

2. How many dogs did John have? What breed were they?
이웃은 몇 마리의 애완견을 길렀나? 혈통은 무엇이었나?

3. What caused Nasser to bark and run to the road?
나세르가 짖어대며 길 쪽으로 달려 나간 이유는 무엇이었나?

4. How did the dogs show loyalty?
애완견들은 어떤 식으로 자신들의 충직함을 보여주었나?

Translation

그날은 사상 최고의 무더위로 기록될 정도로 뜨거웠던 어느 여름날이었다. 스티브 스미스의 집을 둘러싼 나무들에게서는 예전의 그 파릇파릇한 기운을 전혀 찾아 볼 수가 없었는데, 그도 그럴 것이 여러 달째 비가 내리지 않았기 때문이었다. 그런 무더위에도 아랑곳하지 않고 스티브의 이웃은 그의 두 마리 검은 래브(래브라도리트리버)들과 매일 조깅을 했다. 스티브의 이웃 존처럼 그 두 마리 검은 래브도 사교성이 좋아서 때때로 스티브 집에 들러서는 스티브의 맹견 나세르와 어울려 놀기도 했다.

어느 날 부엌에 있던 스티브는 나세르가 현관문을 향해 필사적으로 짖어대는 소리를 들었다. 그가 현관문을 열어 주자, 나세르는 쏜살같이 달려 나가 앞 뜰 안에서 기다리고 있던 두 마리 검은 래브와 만났다. 합세한 세 마리 개들은 길 쪽으로 질주해 나갔고, 길 위에 쓰러져 있는 존을 향해 요란하게 짖어댔다. 그는 죽은 것만 같았다. 그 소란을 들은 또 다른 이웃이 무슨 일인가 하고 나왔다가 쓰러져 있는 사람을 발견하고는 앰뷸런스를 불렀다.

열사병으로 실신했던 존은 나중에 회복되었다. 세 마리 애완견들은 모두 충성심과 봉사를 보여주어, 스티브와 존을 뿌듯하게 했다.

31 The Hero

영웅 빌라

It was the worst and coldest winter in years, storms would [1]paralyze parts of the country without mercy. Sam Thompson's black lab, named Villa, was kept outside in a doghouse, even during the coldest of winter nights.

At the time, she was a half-grown puppy, and during another severe [2]blizzard, she started to bark from her doghouse. After several minutes, she leapt over the five-foot fence and ran over to the neighbor's yard. The snow was so thick that visibility was zero, and the winds were [3]howling at more than 80km an hour!

Andrea, the eleven-year old girl, who lived next door, had gone outside to watch the storm. At a distance of about 50 meters from her house, she became [4]disoriented, stuck in a snowdrift, and was unable to free herself. Villa heard her cry for help and circled the young girl several times before she could free herself. Then Villa led Andrea safely back to her house. What an awesome dog!

---

1 paralyze 마비시키다 **2 blizzard** 강한 눈보라 **3 howling** 윙윙거리는 **4 disorient** ~에게 길[방향]을 잃게 하다

1. What was the weather like?

어떤 날씨였나?

2. How did the dog get over the fence and why?

빌라는 울타리를 어떻게 넘었으며, 그렇게 한 이유는 무엇이었나?

3. How far away was little Andrea from the house when she became stuck?

안드레아가 눈보라 속에 갇혀 있을 때 집에서 얼마나 떨어져 있었나?

4. How did Villa free the little girl from the snow?

빌라는 어린 소녀가 눈보라 속에서 헤쳐 나올 수 있도록 어떻게 도와주었나?

Translation

그해 겨울은 수년 만에 가장 춥고 혹독했다. 샘 톰슨이 살고 있는 지역에는 폭설까지 내려 마비가 될 정도였다. 7의 검은 래브(래브라도리트리버), 빌라는 매서운 한겨울밤에도 바깥에 있는 개집에서 지냈다.

빌라가 아직 강아지였을 때인 어느 날 눈보라가 심하게 쳤고 개집에 있던 빌라가 짖어대기 시작했다. 몇 분이 지난 후, 빌라는 1.5m 높이의 울타리를 뛰어넘어 이웃집 마당으로 달려갔다. 눈보라가 심해 한지 앞도 보이지 않는데다, 시속 80km기 넘는 강한 바람이 윙윙 소리를 내며 불고 있었다!

이웃에 사는 11세 소녀인 안드레아는 폭설을 구경하기 위해 밖에 나왔다. 그 소녀는 자신의 집에서 50m 떨어진 곳에서 길을 잃고, 강한 눈보라 속에 갇혀 혼자서는 도저히 헤쳐 나오지 못하는 상태였다. 빌라는 도와 달라는 소녀의 외침을 들었고, 소녀가 스스로 헤쳐 나올 수 있을 때까지 소녀 주위를 몇 차례나 선회했다. 그러고 나서 빌라는 안드레아를 안전하게 집까지 안내했다. 대단한 개 아닌가!

32 Buck

아이들의 경호견 벅

Alex Douma's family never had to go looking for a dog. They always just seemed to arrive. The first came at the beginning of a summer when Alex's children were returning home from school.

They excitedly [1]stammered that a dog lay howling in the ditch, just [2]adjacent to their property. Alex was curious to the reason why the dog could not move his [3]hindquarters and just stayed in the [4]slime of the ditch.

Mr. Douma inched down to the dog and let it smell his hand. The dog's gentle eyes [5]allayed any fear of him biting Alex. In a family [6]endeavor, the Doumas returned with a wheelbarrow, and everyone [7]steadied the old brown lab as they brought him home. The excited boys helped hose him down and fed him peanut butter sandwiches and an entire bag of dog chow.

With tears in his eyes, a local veterinarian informed Alex that the dog had twelve pellets of [8]buckshot lodged in his hips, narrowly missing his spine. Due to his age, the pellets were left, but the Doumas were assured that with therapy, they could restore his mobility. Buckshot, then shortened to Buck, became Mr. Douma's sons' constant companion and guardian.

Buck was already [9]deemed very old. To a stranger he looked intimidating and dangerous. However, in actuality, he never growled, and his gentleness was unbelievable for what he had been through. He was grateful, faithful, and ever protective over all the children. Each night, Buck would sleep a little in each child's room, always on guard.

Years later, Buck died on the highway exactly where the Douma family fished him out of the ditch. At the time, he could not hear well, had no teeth, and was losing his sight. A large transport truck ran over Buck as he was following the children home from buying candy at the local store. Buck had strayed out too far on the road. Buck's legacy is that of a loyal and grateful friend, whose devotion and love will always be fondly remembered.

---

1 **stammer** 말을 더듬다　2 **adjacent** 부근의, 이웃한　3 **hindquarters** 개의 뒷다리
4 **slime** 진흙　5 **allay** (공포 · 불안을) 가라앉히다　6 **endeavor** 노력　7 **steady** 흔들리지 않게 하다　8 **buckshot** 사슴 사냥용 총알　9 **deem** ~라는 의견을 가지다, 생각하다

Comprehension Questions

1. Who found the hurt dog?
누가 부상당한 개를 발견했나?

2. What breed of dog was Buck?
벅의 혈통은 무엇인가?

3. How did the family get Buck out of the ditch?
가족들은 벅을 어떻게 도랑에서 건져냈나?

4. How did Buck get his name?
'벅' 이란 이름은 어떻가 붙여졌나?

5. What kind of a dog was Buck?
벅은 어떤 개였나?

6. How and where did Buck die?
벅은 어디서 어떻게 죽었나?

알렉스 다우마 가족은 한 번도 개를 구하러 다닌 적이 없었다. 언제나 개들이 스스로 나타나는 것 같았다. 맨 처음 개가 나타난 것은 어느 초여름 알렉스의 아이들이 학교에서 돌아오던 때였다.

아이들이 흥분하여 더듬거리며 말하기를 집 부근의 도랑에 개 한 마리가 빠져 낑낑거리고 있다는 것이었다. 알렉스는 왜 그 개가 뒷다리를 쓰지 못해 질퍽한 도랑에서 빠져 나오지 못하는지 궁금했다.

다우마 씨는 그 개에게로 조금씩 내려가 손을 내밀어 그 개가 냄새 맡도록 했다. 개의 순한 눈망울을 보자 물지나 않을까 하는 두려움은 사라졌다. 온 가족이 합세하여 바퀴 달린 손수레를 가지고 다시 와서 그 노쇠한 갈색 래브라도를 태워 흔들리지 않게 붙잡고 집으로 데려왔다. 흥분한 아이들은 알렉스를 도와 개에게 호스로 물을 뿌려 씻기고 개에게 땅콩버터 샌드위치와 개 사료가 든 자루를 통째로 주었다.

동네 수의사는 눈물이 그렁그렁한 채 개의 엉덩이에 척추를 살짝 비껴 12개의 탄알이 박혀 있다고 알렉스에게 말해 주었다. 다우마 가족은 개의 나이가 너무 많아 탄알을 제거할 수는 없지만 치료를 받으면 다시 움직이게 할 수는 있다는 말에 안심했다. 벅샷이라 했다가 나중에 벅으로 줄여 부르게 된 이 개는 다우마 씨 아이들의 충실한 벗이자 경호견이 되었다.

벅은 이미 노쇠한 상태였다. 낯선 사람에게는 위협적이고 위험해 보였지만 사실 그는 결코 으르렁대지 않았다. 순탄하지 못한 그의 생을 생각하면 그의 유순함은 놀라운 것이었다. 그는 감사해 했고 충직했으며 아이들 모두를 보호해 주었다. 매일 밤 벅은 아이들 각자의 방을 돌며 조금씩 잠을 자면서 보초를 섰다.

몇 년 후, 벅은 다우마 가족이 그를 건져 낸 도랑이 있는 바로 그 도로 위에서 죽었다. 당시 그는 잘 듣지 못했고, 이빨도 다 빠졌고, 시력도 잃어 가고 있었다. 벅은 동네 가게에서 사탕을 사 가지고 집으로 돌아가던 아이들을 뒤따르다가 그만 대형 트럭에 치이고 말았다. 도로 위로 너무 들어섰던 것이다. 벅이 남기고 한 것은 충실하고 고마운 우정이었으며, 그의 헌신과 사랑은 언제나 다정하게 기억될 것이다.

33 The Loyal Sheepdog

충직한 양치기견 팁

Tip, a sheep dog, and her master, Joseph Tagg, an eighty-one year old, regularly went on long walks. The two of them would disappear for many hours in the forest adjacent to the sheep [1]grazing meadows.

On one such walk on December 12, 1953, Joseph died of a heart attack in the depths of the forest. Winter had set in suddenly, and this particular year, the snow and cold were almost [2]unbearable. Again and again, search parties were unable to find Joseph and his dog. Bad weather was the main reason for the lack of success in finding them. Finally, the man and his dog were [3]presumed dead.

Fifteen weeks later, a couple of men rounding up stray sheep in early spring, came across Joseph's body with a starving and [4]sickly Tip beside it. She had waited for over three months through the worst of winter for help to come for the one she loved.

Tip spent the remainder of her life with Joseph's niece, in Derbyshire, England, where she was awarded the

highest order of canine [5]chivalry. A year after her death,
a memorial shrine was unveiled along the banks of
Derwent Dam, in Derbyshire.

1 grazing meadow (방목용의) 목초지, 초원   **2 unbearable** 참을[견딜] 수 없는
3 presume ~로 간주하다, 믿어버리다   **4 sickly** 생기[활기] 없는   **5 chivalry** 용감한 무사

Comprehension Questions

1. What breed of dog was Tip?
   팁의 혈통은 무엇이었나?

2. Where would Tip and her master frequently go?
   팁과 그의 주인은 자주 어디로 가곤 했나?

3. How did Tip's master die?
   팁의 주인은 어떻게 죽었나?

4. Why were search parties unable to locate the two?
   수색자들은 왜 그 둘을 찾아낼 수 없었나?

5. How long had past before Tip and her master were discovered?
   얼마나 지나서 팁과 그의 주인이 발견되었나?

6. How did the town honor Tip?
   그 도시는 어떤 식으로 팁에게 경의를 표했나?

양치기견 팁과 81세인 그의 주인 조지프 태그는 규칙적으로 장거리 산책을 나갔다. 그 둘은 여러 시간 동안 양들이 풀을 뜯어먹는 초원 곁에 있는 숲속으로 사라지곤 했다.

1953년 12월 12일, 그렇게 산책을 하다가 조지프는 깊은 숲속에서 심장 발작을 일으켜 사망하고 말았다. 한파가 급작스럽게 찾아왔고, 특히 그해의 눈과 추위는 너무나도 견디기 힘들었다. 되풀이된 수색 작업에도 조지프와 그의 애완견을 찾을 수 없었다. 기상 악화가 그들을 찾는 데 실패한 주된 원인이었다. 마침내 조지프와 그의 애완견은 죽었을 것이라고 여겨지게 되었다.

15주가 흐른 초봄에, 남자 둘이 길 잃은 양들을 찾아 한데 모으고 있다가, 우연히 조지프의 사체와 그 옆을 지키고 있는 생기 잃고 허기진 팁을 발견했다. 그 애완견은 3개월 동안이나 혹독한 겨울을 나면서 자기가 사랑한 사람을 구조해 줄 도움의 손길을 기다렸던 것이다.

팁은 여생을 영국의 더비셔에 살고 있는 조지프의 조카와 함께 지냈다. 그리고 그곳에서 팁은 최고의 용맹견상을 수상하였다. 팁이 세상을 떠난 1년 뒤, 기념비가 더비셔에 있는 더웬트 댐의 제방을 끼고 세워졌다.

124

34 The Tale of Greyfriars Bobby

프란체스코 수도회의
충견 보비

This is a tale of the world's most famous Scottish terrier. John Gray and his Scottish terrier, Bobby, came to Edinburgh to work for the police as security guards. Over time, the loyal terrier and his master became very well-known to the local population. They were on a first name basis with all of the shopkeepers, and townspeople alike.

Eight years passed when, unfortunately, John [1]contracted [2]tuberculosis and died. He was buried in Greyfriars Churchyard. Bobby became a street dog without any particular place to live and was [3]permitted to wander in the city, because he had been so well-known. Bobby touched the hearts of local residents when he began to visit his master's grave every night. Neither rain, sleet, snow, nor cold could stop the visits, and as a result, Bobby became famous in Edinburgh.

People would come from far and wide to see the dog visit his master. The mayor of the city even paid for Bobby's dog license and bought him an [4]engraved dog collar with his own silver name tag. Even though dogs weren't allowed in the cemetery, a shelter was built for Bobby beside his master's grave. Bobby continued to visit and be loyal to his master for the next 14 years until his death.

The Baroness, Burdett Coutts, set up a [5]memorial for the dog opposite the graveyard in 1873. You can still see the statue of Bobby in Edinburgh today. The Capital will never forget its most famous and faithful dog.

1 contract (병에) 걸리다 **2 tuberculosis** 결핵 **3 permit** 허락하다, 용인하다
4 engrave (문자·도안을) 새기다 **5 memorial** 기념물

1. **What breed of dog was Bobby?**
   보비의 혈통은 무엇이었나?

2. **How did his master die?**
   그의 주인은 어떻게 죽었나?

3. **How did Bobby touch the hearts of the local townspeople?**
   보비의 어떤 행동에 마을 사람들이 감동했나?

4. **Who paid for Bobby's dog tags?**
   누가 보비에게 개목걸이를 사 주었나?

5. **How long did Bobby live after his master's death?**
   보비는 그의 죽인이 죽고 얼마나 더 살았나?

6. **How did the townspeople honor Bobby's loyalty?**
   마을 사람들은 보비의 충성심을 어떻게 기렸나?

Translation

이것은 전세계적에서 가장 유명한 스코티시테리어에 관한 이야기이다. 존 그레이와 그의 스코티시테리어 보비는 에든버러로 와서 경비를 맡아 경찰서에서 근무했다. 시간이 지나자 충직한 테리어와 그의 주인은 지역 주민들 사이에 아주 유명해졌다. 그 둘은 상점 주인들은 물론 마을 사람들과도 아주 친했다.

8년이란 세월이 흐른 뒤 불행하게도 존은 결핵에 걸려 세상을 떠나고 말았다. 존은 프란체스코 수도회 교회의 뜰에 안치되었다. 보비는 마땅히 실 곳이 없어 떠돌이 신세기 되었다. 그는 유명했기 때문에 시내에서 배회하는 것이 용인되었다. 보비가 매일 밤 주인의 묘를 방문하기 시작하자, 마을 사람들이 감동하게 되었다. 비나 눈 또는 추위도 보비의 방문을 막을 수는 없었다. 그 결과 보비는 에든버러 전역에서 유명해졌다.

주인의 묘를 방문하는 그 애완견을 보러 방방곡곡에서 사람들이 모여들었다. 시장은 보비의 애견 등록비를 대신 지불해 주고, 보비의 이름이 새겨진 은제 이름표가 달린 개목걸이를 선사했다. 묘지 안에는 어떠한 개도 출입할 수 없었지만, 보비를 위한 조그만 개집이 주인의 묘 옆에 세워졌다. 보비는 주인을 계속 찾았고, 세상을 떠날 때까지 14년 동안 주인에게 충성을 다했다.

1873년 버넷 쿠츠 남작 부인이 그 애완견을 위한 기념물을 묘지 반대편에 세웠다. 오늘날에도 에든버러에 가면 프란체스코 수도회 교회에 있는 보비의 동상을 볼 수 있다. 에든버러는 가장 유명하고 충직한 그 애완견을 영원히 기억할 것이다.

35 Woody

벼랑에서 뛰어내려
주인을 구한 우디

Woody was a mixed breed collie, and Ray was her master. They were inseparable, and they loved to hike in the country where the peace and [1]solitude were a welcome change from the [2]bustle of the big city. Ray loved photography and usually took numerous pictures on every [3]excursion.

On one such hike, Woody, Ray and his girlfriend, were enjoying the countryside when Ray carefully inched out on an eighty-foot cliff to take a picture, not noticing the loose rock he was standing on. Suddenly, the rock shifted, and Ray tumbled over the edge. Woody, who was standing right beside Ray, leapt down after him without any [4]hesitation.

When rescuers arrived at the bottom, Woody was beside Ray, [5]nudging his head out from the river water where they had both landed. Both of Ray's legs were broken, and Woody had broken both of her hips in the leap to be with her master. However, both recovered well from the [6]ordeal.

1 solitude 외따로 떨어져 있음, 인적이 없음 **2 bustle** 혼잡, 소란스러움 **3 excursion** 짧은 여행 **4 hesitation** ～하기를 망설임, 주저 **5 nudge** ～을 팔꿈치로 살짝 찌르다, 조금씩 밀다 **6 ordeal** 시련

Comprehension Questions

1. What breed of dog was Woody?
우디의 혈통은 무엇인가?

2. Why did Ray and Woody enjoy hiking?
레이와 우디는 왜 하이킹을 즐겼나?

3. What hobby did Ray have?
레이는 어떤 취미를 가지고 있었나?

4. How did Woody prove her loyalty for her master?
우디는 주인에 대한 자신의 충성심을 어떤 식으로 보여주었나?

5. How were the two injured?
그 둘은 어떻게 부상당했나?

Translation

우디는 잡종 콜리로, 수인은 레이었나. 그 둘은 늘 붙어다녔으며, 인적이 드물고 평화로운 교외로 하이킹 나가는 것을 좋아했다. 그것은 대도시의 혼잡과 북적거림에서 벗어날 수 있는 즐거운 변화였다. 레이는 사진찍기를 좋아해서 아주 짧은 여행에서도 수많은 사진을 찍곤 했다.

여느 때처럼 하이킹을 즐기던 어느 날 우디, 레이, 레이의 여자 친구는 시골 외곽에서 즐거운 한때를 보내고 있었다. 그때 레이는 24m 높이의 절벽 위에서 사진을 찍기 위해 조심스럽게 움직이고 있었다. 자신이 딛고 서 있는 바위가 흔들거린다는 것을 레이는 눈치채지 못했고, 그때 갑자기 바위가 흔들리자 레이는 중심을 잃고 벼랑 끝에서 굴러 떨어졌다. 우디는 레이의 바로 옆에 서 있다가 그가 떨어지자 아무런 망설임도 없이 뒤따라 뛰어내렸다.

구조대원들이 절벽 아래에 도착했을 때, 우디는 주인의 머리를 강물 밖으로 가볍게 밀쳐내고 있었다. 레이의 양쪽 다리가 부러지고, 주인과 함께 뛰어내린 탓으로 우디의 양쪽 엉덩이도 부서졌지만, 그 둘 모두 부상에서 회복되었다.

36 Faith

불굴의 애완견 페이스

The most unusual dog story originates from Oklahoma City and is about a small mixed breed dog by the name of Faith. At three weeks of age, Laura, her owner, picked her out of a [1]litter, because she [2]stood out from the rest of the puppies.

Her legs were not fully developed. Faith could not walk like an ordinary dog. Through [3]sheer [4]determination, over just a few short months, Faith learned to balance her [5]torso on her two hind legs and walk [6]upright. Initially, she balanced herself in a snowdrift and gradually her hindquarters became stronger. She was able to play and even chase cats.

1 **litter** (개 · 돼지 등의) 한배 새끼   2 **stand out** 눈에 띄다   3 **sheer** 순수한, 완전한
4 **determination** 결심, 결의   5 **torso** 몸통   6 **upright** 똑바로

1. **What breed of dog was Faith?**
   페이스의 혈통은 무엇인가?

2. **How was Faith handicapped?**
   페이스는 어떻게 하여 장애를 가지게 되었나?

3. **How did Faith get around?**
   페이스는 어떻게 장애를 극복했나?

4. **What were some of Faith's hobbies?**
   페이스의 취미는 무엇인가?

Translation

가장 유별난 애완견 이야기는 오클라호마 시의 페이스라는 이름을 가진 작은 잡종견에 대한 것일 것이다. 생후 3주가 되었을 때, 주인 로라는 젖을 물고 있던 어미 배에서 그 강아지를 골라냈다. 왜냐하면 그 강아지는 남다른 데가 있었기 때문이었다.

페이스의 양다리는 완전히 발육되지 못하였고, 다른 보통 강아지들처럼 걸을 수도 없었다. 그러나 페이스는 불굴의 의지로 불과 몇 달 만에 자신의 뒷다리로 몸의 균형을 잡고 똑바로 서서 걷는 것을 익혔다. 그 강아지는 눈더미 속에서 처음 스스로 균형을 잡았고, 뒷다리는 점차 강하게 단련되었다. 페이스는 장난을 치거나 심지어 고양이까지 쫓아다닐 수 있게 되었다.

37 Wheely Willy

휠체어를 탄 휠리 윌리

Deborah was [1]haunted by the story of a Chihuahua, who had been found in a cardboard box in the garbage. Its [2]vocal chords had been [3]surgically [4]severed not to make any noise, and its hindquarters were paralyzed because of an accident before it was found. The veterinarian to whom the Chihuahua was brought, decided to find a home for it, because it had such a good [5]disposition and was in no pain. A year went by, before Deborah came to see the dog, and the moment she did, it was mutual love at first sight. She picked up the two-pound dog, took him home, and decided to call him Willy.

Not long after, Deborah read about and ordered a wheelchair for Willy, called a K-9 cart. Willy could not have been happier. He took off like an airplane and raced around with the cart that carried his hindquarters, finally freeing him of the limitations he had so patiently endured. Deborah began taking Willy to the local hospital, where he became an inspiration to children in wheelchairs. Willy became famous almost overnight in

"

Los Angeles. The spirit of this little dog was [6]infectious, and he became known as Wheely Willy.

One year later, at the L.A. marathon, Willy led a group of people in wheelchairs, suffering from spinal chord injuries. His K-9 cart had a heart-shaped sign that read Wheely Willy, Official Mascot.

1 haunted (생각 · 기억 등에) 사로잡힌　**2 vocal chords** 성대　**3 surgical** 수술의　**4 sever** ~을 절단하다　**5 disposition** 성질　**6 infectious** 전염성인

1. What breed of dog was Willy?

윌리의 혈통은 무엇인가?

2. Why did the veterinarian decide to find a home for Willy?

수의사는 왜 윌리에게 집을 찾아 주기로 결심했나?

3. What is a K-9 cart?

K-9 휠체어는 무엇인가?

4. How did Willy get the name Wheely Willy?

윌리는 왜 '휠리 윌리'로 불리게 되었나?

5. Who has Wheely Willy been an inspiration for?

휠리 윌리는 누구에게 용기와 희망을 주었나?

Translation

데보라는 쓰레기통의 널빤지 상자 속에서 발견된 치와와에 대한 이야기에 마음을 빼앗겨 버렸다. 발견 당시 그 강아지의 성대는 수술로 절단되어 어떠한 소리도 낼 수 없었고, 뒷다리는 사고로 인해 마비되어 있었다. 치와와를 발견해 데려온 수의사는 강아지를 위해 집을 찾아 주기로 결심했다. 왜냐하면 그 강아지는 착한 심성을 가지고 있었고 더 이상 아프지도 않았기 때문이었다. 일년 후, 데보라가 그 강아지를 보러 왔을 때 첫눈에 그 둘은 서로 사랑에 빠져 버렸다. 데보라는 1킬로그램도 채 못 되는 강아지를 품에 안아 집으로 돌아왔고, 윌리라는 이름을 붙여 주었다.

얼마 지나지 않아 데보라는 K-9이라는 휠체어에 대한 기사를 읽고는 윌리를 위해 주문했다. 윌리는 매우 행복했다. 그는 마치 비행기처럼 힘차게 휠체어에 뛰어올라 어디든지 달려갈 수 있었다. 휠체어는 윌리로 하여금 그 동안 끈기 있게 참아 왔던 뒷다리에 대한 속박에서 벗어나게 해주었다. 데보라는 윌리를 지역 병원에 데리고 다니기 시작했다. 그곳에서 그는 휠체어를 탄 아이들에게 용기와 희망을 주었다. 윌리는 로스앤젤레스 시에서 하루아침에 유명해졌다. 그 작은 강아지의 정신력은 여러 사람들에게 알려졌고, 그는 휠리 윌리로 알려지게 되었다.

일년 후 LA에서 열린 마라톤 경기에서 윌리는 척추 손상으로 인해 휠체어를 탄 사람들에 앞서 그들을 이끌었다. 그의 K-9 휠체어에는 '대회 공식 마스코트 휠리 윌리'라고 씌어진 심장 모양의 표시가 붙어 있었다.

38 The Loyal Friend

곰과 싸운 용감한 사샤

One cold autumn morning, Jeff Chevalier and his dog, Sasha, were hunting in the woods of Northern Canada. Jeff had decided earlier to take a different dog with him on his hunting excursion, but at the last moment, he changed his mind and took Sasha. This would later prove to be one of the best decisions that he had ever made.

Jeff was hunting rabbit and was hoping that Sasha would [1]scare up a few for Jeff to take aim at and shoot. It had been a while since Jeff had gone hunting, and he enjoyed every minute of the three-hour [2]secluded walk though the rough [3]undulating landscape with his dog.

Jeff had nearly walked in a complete circle through the woods and was about one kilometer away from the hunting camp, where he first started, when Sasha started to act up, growling and running in circles. Jeff, [4]bewildered by his dog's behavior, immediately marched over to the dog and attempted to grab its collar when, suddenly, the ground gave way, and Jeff fell into a shallow underground cave.

Jeff fell into a bear's den. As soon as he realized it, he reached for his gun, but it was too late. A black bear was feeding in the den when Jeff fell through. During the fall, a dazed Jeff dropped his gun and was defenseless.

Snarling with one arm raised, the black bear closed in to attack Jeff. Just then, from above Sasha lunged down into the bear den, attacking the bear's throat as if it were [5]instinct!

Although Sasha was no match for the bear and was easily [6]swatted off, she gave Jeff the seconds he needed to find his gun and take aim at the [7]ferocious beast, ultimately [8]slaying it. The hunting duo escaped with only minor scratches and bruises and a story to tell for years to come. A story about a hunting dog named Sasha that risked her own life to save her master's.

1 **scare up** (숨어 있는 사냥 짐승을) 몰아내다 2 **secluded** 외딴 3 **undulating landscape** 기복이 많은 풍경 4 **bewildered** 당황한 5 **instinct** 본능 6 **swat** 찰싹 때리다 7 **ferocious** 사나운 8 **slay** 죽이다

1. Where did this story take place?
이 이야기는 어디에서 일어났나?

2. What type of animal were the two hunting?
그 둘은 어떤 종류의 동물을 사냥 중이었나?

3. What did Jeff fall into?
제프는 어디로 떨어졌나?

4. How did Sasha risk her own life for her master?
사샤는 주인을 구하기 위해 어떻게 했나?

Translation

찬 기운이 감도는 어느 가을 아침에 제프 슈발리에와 그의 개 사샤는 캐나다 북부 산림에서 사냥을 하고 있었다. 처음에 제프는 이번 사냥 여행에는 다른 개를 데려오려고 하였으나, 마지막 순간에 마음을 바꿔 사샤를 데려왔다. 그리고 그것은 그가 내린 결정 중 최고의 것이었음이 나중에 판명되었다.

제프는 토끼 사냥 중이었고, 자신이 잘 조준해 쏠 수 있도록 사샤가 숨어 있는 짐승들을 쫓아내 주기를 바랐다. 마지막으로 사냥을 한 뒤, 그는 3시간 내내 기복이 심한 풍경을 바라보면서 인적이 없는 곳을 자신의 애완견과 함께 걸었다.

제프가 숲을 거의 일주하여 처음에 사냥을 시작했던 캠프에서 1킬로미터 정도 떨어진 지점에 다다랐을 때였다. 사샤가 예사롭지 않게 마구 짖어대더니 빙빙 돌며 뛰어다녔다. 제프는 사샤의 돌발적인 행동에 당황하여 곧 그에게 다가가 개목걸이를 잡으려고 시도했다. 그러자 그때 땅이 꺼지면서 제프는 얕은 땅굴로 굴러 떨어지고 말았다.

제프는 곰의 굴에 빠진 것이다. 그가 그것을 깨달은 순간 자신의 총을 집기 위해 손을 뻗었으나 때는 이미 늦었다. 제프가 떨어졌을 때 마침 검은색 곰은 새끼에게 젖을 물리고 있는 중이었다. 굴 속에 떨어지면서 당황한 나머지 제프는 총을 떨어뜨렸기 때문에 이제 무방비 상태였다.

곰은 한 팔을 들어 올린 채 으르렁거리며 공격하려고 다가섰다. 바로 그때 위에서 달려든 사샤가 곰굴로 돌진하여 마치 본능처럼 곰의 목덜미를 공격했다.

사샤는 곰의 적수가 되지 못해 단번에 얻어맞고 나가 떨어졌지만, 제프가 총을 집어 들고 사나운 짐승을 겨눌 만한 시간적 여유를 제공했고, 결국 곰을 물리칠 수 있었다. 제프와 사샤는 가벼운 상처만 입은 채 무사히 빠져나올 수 있었고, 목숨을 걸고 주인을 살린 개의 무용담은 여러 해 동안 회자되었다.

39 Scooby's Amazing Trip

During a terrible thunderstorm, a [1]startled dog, named Scooby, snapped free of his collar and ran away from home.

During his midnight travels, the six-year old dog wandered on the road and was struck by a passing car, wounding his leg and tail.

Most injured animals would hide or lie and wait for their owner to find them, but not Scooby. [2]Weary, but full of [3]wit, Scooby somehow decided that he needed medical attention and began his lifesaving [4]trudge to the local veterinarian clinic.

Limping and whimpering in pain all the way, Scooby [5]staggered across a three-lane highway, past several neighborhoods, and made his way to the local veterinarian clinic several miles away before it opened the next morning.

When the workers arrived, they were [6]astonished to see that an injured animal had arrived at the clinic [7]unaided. Even more surprisingly, when the door opened, Scooby

limped into the clinic, past the lobby, right into the
examining room, and awaited treatment.

Dr. Gerald of the Corbin animal clinic contacted
Scooby's owners and successfully treated Scooby's
injuries. The clever canine made a full recovery.

1 **startle** 깜짝 놀라게 하다 2 **weary** 지친, 기진맥진한 3 **wit** 기지, 재치 4 **trudge** 무거운
발걸음으로 걷다, 터벅터벅 걷다 5 **stagger** 비틀거리며 나아가다 6 **astonish** 놀라게 하다
7 **unaided** 도움 없는, 혼자 힘으로

Comprehension Questions

1. **Where did this story take place?**
   이야기가 일어난 곳은 어디인가?

2. **How was Scooby injured? Where?**
   스쿠비는 어디서 어떻게 부상당했나?

3. **How did Scooby arrive at the veterinarian clinic?**
   스쿠비는 어떻게 동물 병원에 도착했나?

4. **Who treated Scooby?**
   누가 스쿠비를 치료했나?

5. **Did Scooby make a full recovery?**
   스쿠비는 완쾌되었나?

Translation

심한 폭풍우가 몰아치던 날, 깜짝 놀란 애완견 스쿠비는 자신의 개목걸이를 끊고는 집에서 도망쳤다.

여섯 살 된 이 애완견은 밤새 돌아다니는 도중 도로 위를 헤매다가 지나가는 차에 치어 다리 하나와 꼬리에 부상을 입었다.

대부분의 부상당한 동물들은 주인이 그들을 찾을 때까지 기다리거나 숨거나 누워 있지만 스쿠비는 그렇지 않았다. 심신은 지쳤지만 총명한 그 개는 어떻게든 치료 받아야겠다고 판단하고는 마을에 있는 동물 병원을 향해 자신의 생명을 구하기 위한 힘겨운 발걸음을 떼기 시작했다.

다리를 절뚝거리고 고통으로 내내 낑낑대면서 스쿠비는 편도 3차선 고속도로를 비틀비틀 건넜고, 몇몇 동네를 지나, 몇 마일이나 떨어진 지역 동물 병원을 찾아갔다. 다음날 아침 동물 병원이 문을 열기 전이었다.

출근한 병원 직원들은 부상을 당한 동물이 사람의 도움 없이 병원 앞에 있는 것을 보고 놀라지 않을 수 없었다. 게다가 더욱 놀라운 사실은 문을 열자 스쿠비가 제 발로 절뚝거리며 병원으로 들어오더니 로비를 지나 검사실로 들어가 치료를 기다렸다는 것이었다.

코빈 동물 병원의 의사 제럴드 박사가 스쿠비의 주인에게 연락을 취했고, 스쿠비의 치료도 성공적이었다. 그 영리한 애완견은 완쾌되었다.

사랑에 빠진 시로

Mr. and Mrs. Nakamura had just moved from Zamami, a small island in Southern Japan, to Aka, a smaller neighboring island 4 kilometers away, with their dog Shiro.

Shiro appeared to be [1]depressed and lonely for the first few days after the move and disappeared early one morning. Later that night, Mr. Nakamura heard a scratch at the door and opened it to see Shiro wet and [2]shivering.

Shiro began to disappear frequently and return again around the same time every evening. This puzzled Mr. Nakamura, so he set out to follow Shiro early one morning.

Shiro [3]snuck away to the beach, entered the water, and began swimming. A [4]curious Mr. Nakamura followed in his boat from a distance. After swimming a distance of nearly 2 kilometers, Shiro climbed onto a large rock and rested for a while before reentering the water again. It was not long before Shiro arrived at Aka, the island where he once lived with the Nakamura family.

Shiro shook off the water and made his way toward town as a very [5]inquisitive Mr. Nakamura followed.

Shiro was met by his girlfriend Marilyn, and the two dogs played together all afternoon!

When Mr. Nakamura told the villagers about Shiro, the story [6]captured the hearts of everyone, and Shiro quickly became famous.

During warmer holidays in Japan, as many as three thousand people [7]flock to the islands of Zamami and Aka to see if Shiro, the dog in love, will swim to his girlfriend one more time.

1 depressed 의기소침한, 우울한 **2 shiver** (추위로) 와들와들 떨다 **3 sneak** 몰래 움직이다
4 curious 호기심 있는 **5 inquisitive** 호기심 많은, 알고 싶어하는 **6 capture the hearts of everyone** 모든 사람들의 마음과 관심을 끌다 **7 flock** 몰려들다, 모이다

Comprehension Questions

1. Where does this story take place?
이것은 어느 곳의 이야기인가?

2. Where does Shiro live?
시로는 어디에 살고 있나?

3. Where does Shiro's girlfriend live?
시로의 여자 친구는 어디에 살고 있나?

4. How does Shiro get to Zamami?
시로는 자마미 섬까지 어떻게 가나?

5. How far is it from Zamami to Aka?
자마미 섬과 아카 섬은 얼마나 떨어져 있나?

6. Why does Shiro swim to Zamami?
시로가 자마미 섬까지 헤엄쳐 간 이유는 무엇인가?

나카무라 부부는 일본 남쪽에 위치한 작은 자마미 섬에서 그 옆에 있는 더 작은 아카 섬으로 애완견 시로와 함께 이사했다. 아카 섬은 자마미 섬으로부터 4킬로미터 떨어진 곳에 있었다.

시로는 이사 후 처음 며칠 동안 외롭고 우울해 보이더니 어느 날 아침 일찍 사라져 버렸다. 그리고 그날 밤에 나카무라 씨는 문을 할퀴는 소리를 들었다. 문을 열어 보니, 문 앞에서 시로가 물에 흠뻑 젖어 와들와들 떨고 있었다.

시로는 자주 사라졌다가 같은 날 저녁 그 시각에 돌아오곤 했다. 이것을 수상히 여긴 나카무라 씨는 어느 날 아침 일찍 시로를 미행하기로 결심했다.

시로는 해변에서 눈치를 보며 시성대다가 물속으로 들어가시는 머리를 수면 위로 내밀고 헤엄치기 시작했다. 호기심이 발동한 나카무라 씨는 자신의 보트를 타고 시로와 거리를 두면서 쫓아갔다. 거의 2킬로미터 정도를 헤엄친 후에 시로는 커다란 바위 위로 올라가서는 잠시 동안 쉬었다가 다시 물속으로 들어갔다. 시로는 오래가지 않아 자마미 섬에 도착했다. 그곳은 예전에 시로가 나카무라 부부와 함께 살던 섬이었다. 시로는 물 밖으로 나와 몸을 털고 나서 시내로 향했다. 나카무라 씨는 너무 궁금한 나머지 그를 뒤따랐다.

시로는 여자 친구 매릴린을 만났고, 그 둘은 오후 내내 함께 놀았다!

나카무라 씨가 마을 사람들에게 시로에 대한 이야기를 하자, 그 이야기는 모두의 마음을 사로잡았고, 시로는 금세 유명해졌다.

일본에서는 따사로운 휴일이면 사랑에 빠진 시로가 여자 친구를 찾아 다시 헤엄쳐 가는지 보기 위해 3천 명이나 되는 사람들이 자마미 섬과 아카 섬으로 모여든다.

There are 701 types of recognized purebred dogs in the world today. Each dog breed has its own character and physical traits, making it unique from the others. During the course of history there have been many outstanding canines and volumes of information written about our four-legged companions. This factual information was collected and compiled from various books, newspaper articles, and Internet resources. Below is a list of canine trivia comprising of 5 different categories and, it also, includes several quizzes to test your knowledge of the world's oldest pet.

오늘날 전세계에는 701종의 순종 개가 있다. 각각의 품종은 저마다 고유의 정신적 · 신체적인 특징을 지니고 있다. 역사를 보면, 개에 관한 이야기들이 많이 있다. 이 책에서 다루게 될 개에 관한 상식은 다양한 책, 신문 기사, 인터넷 자료에서 발췌한 것으로, 5가지 주제로 분류하여 소개하고자 한다. 또한 퀴즈를 통해 인간의 가장 오래된 애완동물인 개에 대해 얼마나 알고 있는지 확인해 보자.

4

Amazing Canine Trivia

개에 대한 흥미로운 사실

41 Physiological Dog Trivia

생리학적·신체적 특징

1. The tallest breed of dog is the Irish Wolfhound.
    가장 키가 큰 품종은 아이리시 울프하운드이다.

2. Dalmatians are born pure white. They are not born with spots.
    달마시안은 점박이지만, 태어날 때는 순백색이다.

3. The smallest breed of dog is the Chihuahua, weighting 2-6 lbs.
    가장 키가 작은 품종은 치와와로서 몸무게가 0.9~2.7kg이다.

4. The Basenji dog breed doesn't bark.
    바센지 종은 짖지 않는다.

5. The Newfoundland breed of dogs have webbed feet, making them great swimmers.
    뉴펀들랜드 종은 발에 갈퀴가 있어 뛰어난 수영 실력을 자랑한다.

6. The Basset hound breed is the only dog that can't swim.
    바셋하운드는 수영을 하지 못하는 유일한 품종이다.

7. Dogs only sweat from the bottoms of their paws. Panting only releases heat.
    개는 발바닥에서만 땀이 난다. 헐떡거리면서 열을 식힌다.

8. The dog's sense of smell is the keenest in nature.
    개는 동물 중 가장 예민한 후각을 가지고 있다.

9. Dogs can see color. They can distinguish between
   blue, yellow, and gray.
   개는 색맹이 아니다. 파랑, 노랑, 회색을 구별할 수 있다.

10. Most dogs have about 100 different facial
    expressions. Most of them are made with the ears.
    대부분의 개는 약 100가지의 다양한 얼굴 표정을 지을 수 있다. 대개는 귀를 이용한다.

11. Dogs have a total of 42 teeth. Cats have 32.
    개는 42개의 이빨을 가지고 있다. 고양이의 이빨 수는 32개이다.

12. The average top speed of the domesticated dog is
    32km/h, but the greyhound breed can reach speeds
    of up to 70km/h.
    길들인 개의 평균 최고 속도는 시속 32km이지만 그레이하운드는 시속 70km에 육박한다.

13. Greyhounds have better eyesight than any other
    breed of dog.
    그레이하운드는 시력이 가장 좋다.

14. There are 701 types of pure breed dogs.
    전세계에는 701종의 순종이 있다.

15. Tests conducted by the University of Michigan
    concluded that a dog's memory lasts no more than 5
    minutes.
    미시간 대학에서 실시한 실험 결과에 따르면, 개의 기억력은 5분을 넘지 못한다고 한다.

16. Dogs have only 10 different vocal sounds. Cats have
    approximately 100.
    개들은 10가지의 소리밖에 낼 수 없다. 고양이는 거의 100가지의 소리를 낼 수 있다.

17. Alaskan sled dogs burn 10,000 calories daily during
    races.
    알래스카의 썰매 끄는 개는 경주 중에 매일 10,000칼로리를 소비한다.

18. Chocolate contains theobromine, a poison that
stimulates the central nervous system and cardiac
muscles in dogs. Just 146g is enough to kill a 22kg
dog.

초콜릿에는 테오브로민이 들어 있다. 이것은 개의 중앙 신경 체계와 심장 근육을 자극하기 때문에 개에게는 독이다. 초콜릿 146g 정도만으로도 22kg에 달하는 개에게 치사량이 될 수 있다.

19. The Pharaoh Hound breed is the only dog that will
blush when excited or happy.

파라오하운드는 흥분하거나 기분이 좋을 때 얼굴이 붉어지는 유일한 개이다.

20. Female dogs carry their babies for approximately 60
days before giving birth.

개의 수태 기간은 약 60일이다.

21. A normal dog's heart will beat 70-120 times per
minute.

보통 개의 심장 박동수는 분당 70~120회이다.

42 Historical Dog Trivia

역사 및 일화

1. The American foxhound is the oldest American breed of dog dating back to 1650.

   미국에서 가장 오래된 품종은 아메리칸폭스하운드로서 그 역사는 1650년으로까지 거슬러 올라간다.

2. On April 25, 1938, the first seeing-eye dog was presented to a blind person.

   1938년 4월 25일에 최초의 맹인견이 맹인에게 인도되었다.

3. The first dog to star in an American movie was a dog named Jean, a Border Collie mix, who made his first film in 1910.

   최초로 미국 영화에 출연한 개는 잡종 보더콜리인 진이다. 진은 1910년에 최초로 영화에 출연했다.

4. In the original 101 Dalmatians movie, the dog Pongo had 72 spots.

   원작 영화 〈101마리의 달마시안〉에 출연한 퐁고에게는 72개의 점이 박혀 있었다.

5. The oldest dog breed is the Saluki, dating back to 3000 BC.

   가장 오래된 품종은 살루키로서 기원전 3000년 전까지 거슬러 올라간다.

6. Before a law was passed in 1978, making it mandatory for owners to clean up after their pets, roughly 40 million pounds of dog excrement were deposited on

the streets of New York, yearly.

애완견 배설물 처리를 주인에게 강제하는 법이 1978년에 통과되기 전까지만 해도 뉴욕의 거리에는 해마다 4천만 파운드(1800만 킬로그램)의 배설물이 노상에 방치되었다.

7. **Two dogs survived the sinking of Titanic, escaping on early deployed lifeboats No.7 and No.3.**

침몰한 타이타닉호에서 두 마리의 개가 생존했다. 그들은 일찍 바다에 내려진 7번 구명 보트와 3번 구명 보트를 타고 있었다.

8. **Walt Disney's family dog was a poodle named Lady.**

월트 디즈니 가족의 애견은 레이디라는 푸들이었다.

9. **Laika, a Russian dog, became the world's first canine to enter space in 1957.**

러시아 개인 라이카는 1957년 세계 최초로 우주를 여행한 개가 되었다.

10. **In 1785, dogs were used to test human parachutes.**

1785년에 개들이 낙하산 시험용으로 이용되었다.

43 Dog Behavior and Nutritional Trivia

행동, 건강, 영양

1. Female dog bites are twice as common as male dog bites. 암컷이 수컷보다 두 배 이상 많이 문다.

2. To urinate, male dogs do not need to lift their legs. 오줌을 눌 때 수컷이 꼭 다리를 들 필요가 있는 것은 아니다.

3. Experiments have shown that some breeds of dogs can locate the source of sound in 6/100ths of a second. 실험 결과에 의하면 일부 품종은 6/100초 이내에 소리가 나는 곳을 찾아낼 수 있다.

4. Turning on the TV for your dog while away is a healthy way to deal with depression and boredom for your dog. 주인이 외출하면서 텔레비전을 켜두는 것이 애완견의 우울증과 지루함을 방지하는 좋은 방법이다.

5. The majority of dogs need interaction to exercise. They will not exercise independently. 대부분의 개는 운동하기 위해 상호 작용이 필요하다. 독자적으로는 운동하려 하지 않는다.

6. It is not necessary to include vitamin C in your dog's diet. As a carnivore, it produces vitamin C naturally. 개 사료에 비타민 C가 꼭 포함되지 않아도 된다. 개는 육식동물로서 비타민 C를 체내 생산한다.

7. The most common dietary problem suffered by canines in America is obesity. 미국에서 개에게 가장 흔한 섭생 문제는 비만이다.

44 Dogs and the Human Connection

1. In North America, the most popular name for a dog is Max.

   북아메리카에서 인기가 가장 높은 개 이름은 맥스이다.

2. Dogs have over 220 million scent receptors in their noses. Humans have only 5 million.

   개들은 코에 2억 2000만 개에 달하는 냄새 수용기를 가지고 있다. 반면에 인간은 500만 개에 불과하다.

3. Dogs only have approximately 1,700 taste buds on their tongues. Humans have roughly 9,000.

   개는 혀에 약 1700개의 맛을 식별할 수 있는 돌기가 있다. 인간은 약 9000개를 가지고 있다.

4. According to the American Red Cross, 33% of dog owners talk to their dogs on the phone or leave messages on an answering machine while away.

   미국 적십자사에 의하면, 애완견 주인의 33%가 외출 중에 개에게 전화를 걸거나 자동 응답기에 메시지를 남긴다고 한다.

5. An estimated 1 million dogs in the United States have been named the primary beneficiary in their owner's will.

   미국에서는 약 100만 마리의 개가 유언의 1차 수혜자로 지정되었다.

6. There are 58 million dogs kept as pets in America, second only to the cat that totals nearly 66 million.

Cats are the number one pets worldwide.

미국의 애완견 수는 5800만 마리에 달하여 6600만 마리에 달하는 고양이에 이어 두 번째이다. 전세계에서 가장 수가 많은 애완동물은 고양이이다.

7. Every year, Americans spend $1.5 billion on pet food. This is four times the amount spent on baby food.

매년 미국인들은 애완동물 사료에 15억 달러를 소비한다. 이는 유아식의 4배에 이르는 수치이다.

8. 94% of those surveyed say that their dog makes them smile at least once a day.

설문 조사의 응답자 가운데 94%가 애완견 덕분에 적어도 하루에 한 번 이상 웃는다고 응답했다.

9. Scientists claim that certain dogs can smell the presence of autism in children.

어떤 개들은 어린이의 자폐증 여부를 냄새로 알아낼 수 있다고 과학자들은 주장한다.

10. Dogs and humans are the only two mammals with prostates.

개와 인간만이 전립선을 가지고 있는 포유동물이다.

11. According to the American Animal Hospital Association, 78% of pet owners sign their pet's names on greeting cards.

미국동물병원협회에 따르면, 애완견 주인의 78%가 연하장에 애완견의 이름을 적는다고 한다.

12. According to the American Animal Hospital Association, 58% of pet owners include their pets in holiday and family portraits.

미국동물병원협회에 따르면, 애완견 주인의 58%가 휴가 여행이나 가족 사진 촬영에 애완견을 포함시킨다고 한다.

13. 39% of pet owners surveyed say that they have more pictures of their pet than of their spouse.

설문 조사에 응답한 39%의 애완견 주인은 배우자보다 애완견의 사진을 더 많이 갖고 있다고 응답했다.

14. In North America, the most popular dog for a pet is the Labrador Retriever.

북아메리카에서 인기가 가장 높은 애완견은 래브라도리트리버이다.

15. A human bite is more infectious than that of a dog.

인간이 문 상처가 개가 문 상처보다 전염성이 높다.

16. 70% of British dogs receive Christmas gifts from their owners.

영국의 개 가운데 70%가 주인으로부터 크리스마스 선물을 받는다.

17. Approximately 4,000 dogs served in the Vietnam War.

약 4000 마리의 개가 베트남 전쟁에 참전했다.

45 Other Odd Dog Facts and Trivia

1. Over 1 million stray dogs live in the New York City metropolitan area.

   뉴욕시 주변에는 약 100만 마리 이상의 집 없는 개가 배회하고 있다.

2. In the early 1940's, Velcro was invented by a Swiss man after noticing all of the burdocks that stuck to his dog during a walk though the woods.

   1940년대 초반, 한 스위스 남자가 자신의 개와 숲속을 산책하는 도중 개에게 들러붙은 우엉의 가시에서 영감을 얻어 벨크로를 발명했다.

3. Smiling at a dog may cause it to attack. Dogs see teeth as a sign of aggression.

   개에게 미소를 지으면 공격을 당할 수 있다. 개는 이를 드러내면 자기를 공격하는 것으로 받아들인다.

4. The Boxer breed of dog was so named for how it fights. When attacking it jabs with its front paws like a human boxer.

   복서라는 품종의 이름은 그것이 싸우는 모습에서 유래되었다. 공격할 때 앞발을 들고 권투 선수처럼 때린다.

5. Based on an average life span of 11 years, the cost of owning a dog is US$13,350.

   애완견의 수명을 평균 11년이라고 할 경우 애완견을 키우는 데는 1만 3350달러의 비용이 든다.

6. According to a study at the Institute for the Study of

Animal Problems in Washington D.C., dogs, like people, are either right-handed or left-handed.
미국 수도 워싱턴에 소재한 동물문제연구소의 연구 결과에 따르면, 개도 사람처럼 왼손잡이거나 오른손잡이라고 한다.

7. The domesticated dog is mentioned 14 times in the bible.
성경에는 사육견에 관한 내용이 열네 번 나온다.

8. Due to a large population of stray animals in the US, each animal shelter puts approximately 30,000 dogs and cats to sleep, yearly.
미국에서는 유기되는 애완동물의 수가 많아 매년 동물 보호소마다 약 3만 마리의 개와 고양이를 죽이고 있다.

9. Scent trails performed by proven Bloodhounds are admissible in some US courts.
그 능력이 입증된 블러드하운드가 맡은 냄새는 미국의 여러 법정에 증거로 제출할 수 있다.

10. The Canary Islands were named after a breed of dogs, not Canary birds.
카나리아 제도의 이름은 카나리아 새가 아니라 카나리아라는 개의 품종명을 딴 것이다.

11. Every known dog breed except the Chow breed has a pink tongue. The Chow's tongue is black.
차우 품종을 제외한 개의 모든 품종은 분홍빛 혀를 가지고 있다. 차우의 혀는 검정색이다.

12. The Star Wars movie character Chewbacca was inspired by George Lucas's Alaskan Malamute.
영화 〈스타워즈〉에 나오는 추바카는 조지 루카스의 애견인 알래스카맬러뮤트에서 아이디어를 얻은 것이다.

46 The Canine Trivia Quiz

퀴즈

How well have you been reading? The following quiz is comprised of 20 trivia questions from each of the 5 different trivia categories. Good luck!

개에 대해서 얼마나 더 알게 되었는가? 앞의 내용에서 20개의 문제가 제시된다. 행운이 있기를!

A. Test your dog trivia by correctly answering TRUE (T) or FALSE (F) for the statements below.

다음 진술을 읽고 맞으면 T, 틀리면 F를 써 넣으시오.

1. Dogs are the most popular pets in North America. (   )

   개는 북아메리카에서 인기가 가장 높은 애완동물이다.

2. A human bite is more infectious than that of a dog. (   )

   인간이 문 상처가 개가 문 상처보다 전염성이 높다.

3. The oldest breed of dog is the American foxhound. (   )

   미국에서 가장 오래된 품종은 아메리칸폭스하운드이다.

4. An estimatcd 1 million dogs will inherit all of their master's possessions after death. (   )

   미국에서 약 100만 마리의 개가 주인이 죽은 후 그의 재산을 모두 상속한다.

5. Dogs sweat by panting. (   )
개는 헐떡거리면서 땀을 흘린다.

6. Dogs, humans, and monkeys are the only animals with prostates. (   )
개, 인간, 그리고 원숭이만이 전립선을 가지고 있는 동물이다.

7. Dalmatians are born pure white. (   )
달마시안은 태어날 때는 순백색이다.

8. In 1978, a law was passed in NY City making it mandatory to clean up after your pet. (   )
1978년에 뉴욕시에서 애완동물 배설물 처리법이 통과되었다.

9. Dogs have roughly ten different vocal sounds. (   )
개는 대략적으로 열 가지의 목소리를 낼 수 있다.

10. Based on the average life span of 11 years, the cost of owning a dog is US$23,000. (   )
애완견의 수명을 평균 11년이라 할 때, 애완견을 키우는 데 2만 3000달러의 비용이 든다.

B. Test your dog trivia by answering the following questions correctly.
다음 질문에 답하시오.

1. What dog inspired the Star Wars character Chewbacca?
〈스타워즈〉에 나오는 추바카란 캐릭터가 나오게 된 배경은 무엇인가?

2. What is the most common name given to dogs in North America?
북아메리카에서 가장 많이 사용되는 애완견의 이름은 무엇인가?

3. How many canines served in the Vietnam War?
베트남 전쟁에 참전한 개는 몇 마리인가?

4. How many teeth do dogs have?
개는 몇 개의 이빨을 가지고 있는가?

5. What is the only breed of dog that cannot swim?
수영을 하지 못하는 유일한 개의 품종은 무엇인가?

6. Due to an overpopulation of stray animals,
approximately how many pets are put to sleep each
year in animal shelters across America?
유기되는 동물의 수가 급증함에 따라 미국 전역에 걸쳐 매년 동물 보호소에서 처리되는 애
완동물은 몇 마리인가?

7. According to the Animal Hospital Association, what
percentage of pet owners sign their pets' names on
greeting cards?
미국 동물병원협회에 따르면 애완견 주인 중 몇 퍼센트가 연하장에 애완견의 이름을 적
는가?

8. What is the most popular dog kept as a pet in North
America?
북아메리카에서 인기가 가장 높은 애완견은 어떤 품종인가?

9. How many different vocal sounds do dogs have?
개는 몇 가지 종류의 소리를 낼 수 있는가?

10. What breed was Walt Disney's family dog?
월트 디즈니 가족의 애견은 어떤 품종이었나?

A.

1. False

   (There are 58 million dogs and nearly 66 million cats.)

2. True

3. False

   (The oldest known breed of dog is the Saluki, dating back to 3000 BC.)

4. True

5. False

   (Dogs only sweat from the bottom of their paws. Panting only releases heat.)

6. False

   (Dogs and humans are the only animals with prostates.)

7. True

8. True

9. True

10. False

    (Based on the average life span of 11 years, the cost of owning a dog is US$13,350.)

B.

1. The character of Chewbacca was inspired by George Lucas's Alaskan Malamute.

2. Max

3. 4,000

4. 42

5. The Basset Hound

6. Approximately 30,000 cats and dogs

7. 78%

8. The Labrador Retriever

9. 10

10. Poodle

47 What is Your Dog Trying to Tell You?

개가 무슨 말을 하려는
것일까?

If you have ever owned a pet, you probably are well aware of the many wacky and often hilarious antics that are preformed in front of your eyes on a daily basis. Knowing what an animal is trying to tell you through behavior can be invaluable. Below is a comical, but informative quiz, challenging you and your knowledge of canine behavior. Good luck!

애완동물을 키워 봤다면 아마도 매일 같이 당신의 눈앞에서 벌어지는 그들의 이상하고 때로는 웃음이 나는 기괴한 짓에 대해 잘 알고 있을 것이다. 그런 행동을 통해 그들이 말하고자 하는 것이 무엇인지를 아는 것은 매우 요긴하다. 익살스럽지만 유익한 다음 퀴즈를 풀면서 개에 대해 얼마나 알고 있는지 알아보기 바란다. 행운이 있기를!

Question 1.

A strange dog is slowly approaching you. As he walks closer to you, you notice that he is staring directly into your eyes. His ears and tail are standing up straight. He is on his tiptoes. The dog's tail is slowly wagging back and forth. What is he trying to tell you?

① I am scared.

② I am friendly.

③ I may bite you.

④ I want to play.

⑤ I am interested in you.

낯선 개가 천천히 당신에게 접근해 오고 있다. 그 개는 가까이 다가오며, 귀와 꼬리를 세우고 발꿈치를 든 채 당신을 똑바로 쳐다본다는 것을 느낄 수 있다. 또한 꼬리를 천천히 앞뒤로 흔든다. 그 개는 무슨 말을 하려는 것일까?

① 무서워요.
② 나는 상냥한 개랍니다.
③ 당신을 물지도 몰라요.
④ 장난치고 싶어요.
⑤ 당신에게 관심 있어요.

Question 2.

An unfamiliar dog approaches you, gently puts his mouth around your hand, and slightly applies pressure. What is this dog trying to tell you?

① I want to go home. I am lost.

② Don't move or I'll bite your hand.

③ I am worried.

④ Hello!

⑤ I am hungry.

낯선 개가 당신에게 다가와서 그의 입을 당신의 손에 놓고 살짝 누른다. 무슨 말을 하려는 것일까?

① 집에 가고 싶어요, 길을 잃었어요.
② 움직이지 마세요, 안 그러면 당신의 손을 물 거예요.
③ 걱정이 있어요.
④ 안녕하세요!
⑤ 배가 고파요.

Question 3.

Your young puppy has just peed on the floor. When you approach, the young dog rolls over and does it once again. What is your dog trying to tell you?

① I like to pee in this spot because of the nice smell.

② I am spiteful. I am doing it again just to anger you and show you who the boss really is.

③ I am submissive. I give up!

④ I don't know the difference between inside and outside.

⑤ I am not housebroken. Please train me.

당신의 개가 바닥에 막 오줌을 쌌다. 당신이 다가가자, 그 강아지는 등을 바닥에 대고 구르기를 반복한다. 무슨 말을 하려는 것일까?

① 이곳의 냄새가 좋기 때문에 여기서 오줌을 누고 싶어요.

② 나는 계속 오줌을 싸서 당신을 화나게 할 거예요. 어디 한번 누가 주인인지 가려 보자고요.

③ 항복! 내가 졌어요!

④ 안이나 밖이나 무슨 차이가 있는 거죠?

⑤ 아직 배변 훈련이 안 됐거든요, 훈련시켜 주세요.

Question 4.

Your seemingly normal male dog mounts another male. {OR} Your female dog just mounted another female. What is going on?

① This is happening because your animal is gay.

② Your dog might have mistakenly eaten some cat food and has gone temporarily crazy.

③ Your dog needs to mate and is frustrated.

④ He wants to show the other dog who is boss.

⑤ **Your dog is just playing with the other dog.**

정상적인 수컷인데 또 다른 수컷 위에 올라탄다. 또는 정상적인 암컷인데 또 다른 암컷 위에 올라탄다. 무슨 일이 벌어지고 있는 것일까?

① 당신의 개는 동성 연애를 하고 있다.
② 당신의 개가 실수로 고양이 사료를 먹어 한동안 제정신이 아니다.
③ 당신의 개가 발정을 해야 하는데 마음대로 되지 않아 좌절했다.
④ 당신의 개는 누가 주도권을 쥐고 있는지 보여주기를 원한다.
⑤ 그저 다른 개와 놀고 있는 중이다.

Question 5.

You have just given a command to your dog to "stay" and you begin to walk away. While you are walking away from your dog, you notice that he is yawning. What is your dog trying to tell you?

① I want a new master.
② I am nervous.
③ I need a walk or some exercise.
④ I am tired, and I think I will have a little nap.
⑤ I am bored to death with you and your commands.

방금 개에게 그대로 있으라고 명령한 후 몇 발자국 걸어 나왔다. 몇 발자국 걸어 나오니까 개가 하품을 한다. 무슨 말을 하려는 걸까?

① 새로운 주인을 원해요.
② 지금 떨려요.
③ 나는 산책 또는 운동이 필요해요.
④ 지금 피곤하니까 낮잠을 조금 자야겠어요.
⑤ 당신과 당신의 명령을 따르기가 지겨워 죽겠어요.

You are trying to teach your dog a few new tricks or commands. After a while of learning, your dog suddenly begins to scratch his neck feverishly. Why is your dog scratching, and what is he trying to tell you?

① I need a break.
② I do not want to learn from you anymore.
③ I am just itchy.
④ Please take my collar off. It feels constricting.
⑤ I have fleas. Can't you see?

개에게 새로운 명령을 훈련시키려고 한다. 훈련을 조금 하더니 갑자기 개가 목을 심하게 긁기 시작한다. 왜 목을 긁는 것이며, 무슨 말을 하려는 것일까?

① 좀 쉬어야겠어요.
② 더 이상 당신한테 배우고 싶지 않아요.
③ 가려워요.
④ 개줄을 풀어 주세요, 숨이 막혀요.
⑤ 벼룩이 있어요, 보이지 않으세요?

You discover that your dog is misbehaving, and you punish him by yelling at him. Your dog will not make cyc contact with you, and his ears are turned backward resting flat on his head. When you approach, your dog licks his lips and avoids you further. What is your dog trying to tell you?

① I am stubborn, and I don't want anything to do with you.
② I surrender! I am sorry!

③ I am depressed and tired of my life.

④ I am not remorseful for anything that I have done.

⑤ I am terrified that you will hit me.

개가 못된 짓을 해서 큰 소리로 야단을 치고 있는 상황이다. 개는 당신을 똑바로 보지 못하고 뒤쪽으로 젖혀진 귀는 머리에 달라붙어 있다. 당신이 다가가면 입맛을 다시면서 당신을 피한다. 무슨 말을 하려는 걸까?

① 나는 고집이 세요. 당신과는 아무것도 하고 싶지 않아요.
② 내가 졌어요! 잘못했어요!
③ 나는 우울해요, 내 삶에 지쳐 버렸어요.
④ 내가 한 행동에 대해 아무런 후회도 없어요.
⑤ 나를 때릴까봐 무서워요.

Question 8.

Walking around your neighborhood, you come across a strange dog. The dog bares teeth and begins to snarl at you. The hair on his back is raised while his tail is held low and stiff. The dog's ears are also flat and turned backward on his head. What is this dog saying?

① You are in my neighborhood. Get out!

② I am sick.

③ I am afraid of you. I may bite or run.

④ I am going to eat you for lunch.

⑤ Let's play.

동네에서 산책하다 낯선 개와 마주친다. 그 개는 이빨을 드러내더니 으르렁거리기 시작한다. 꼬리는 아래로 향해 있는데 경직되어 있고, 등의 털도 뻣뻣이 서 있다. 귀는 뒤쪽으로 젖혀진 상태에서 머리 쪽에 납작하게 붙어 있다. 무슨 말을 하려는 것일까?

① 내 구역이야, 빨리 나가!
② 아파요.
③ 당신이 무서워서 물거나 도망갈지도 몰라요.
④ 당신은 오늘 내 점심거리야.
⑤ 같이 놀아요.

Your dog begins to snort and chatter his teeth. What is your dog trying to tell you?

① I smell a skunk.
② I feel carsick, and I am going to puke.
③ Turn on the heat.
④ I smell a female dog in heat.
⑤ Please feed me.

당신의 개가 콧김을 내품으며 이빨을 덜덜 떨고 있다. 무슨 말을 하려는 것일까?

① 스컹크의 냄새를 맡았어요.
② 자동차 멀미를 하나 봐요. 토할 것 같아요.
③ 추워요, 히터를 켜 주세요.
④ 발정기 암컷의 냄새를 맡았어요.
⑤ 배고파요, 밥 주세요.

Your dog approaches you panting. She begins to bark in a high-pitched tone and bows down before you with her tail wagging. What is your dog trying to tell you?

① I am pregnant, and I don't know who the father is.
② Let's chase a cat.
③ Please play with me.
④ I want some food or water.
⑤ I need to go outside.

당신의 개가 헉헉거리며 당신에게 다가온다. 날카로운 고성으로 짖기 시작하며 꼬리를 세차게 흔들면서 당신 앞에 고개를 숙인다. 무슨 말을 하려는 걸까?

① 임신을 했는데, 애 아빠가 누구인지 모르겠어요.
② 고양이를 쫓아가요.
③ 나와 놀아 주세요.
④ 음식이나 물을 원해요.
⑤ 밖에 나가야 해요.

1. ③ **I may bite you.** (당신을 물지도 몰라요.)

This is a very dominant animal. He has a purpose, and it may be to attack. He is approaching you on his tiptoes, because he is ready to pounce and attack. His tail is wagging slowly, because he is collecting balance. Do not approach such an animal, and don't smile! If you smile, you might show your teeth, and the dog will understand this as aggression. You should turn half away (not fully) and speak in a soft tone while slowly backing away.

이 개는 굉장히 지배력이 강한 놈이다. 목적을 가지고 있고 공격 태세를 갖추고 있다. 발꿈치를 들고 당신에게 다가가는 것은 언제든지 당신에게 달려들 수 있다는 표시이다. 또한 꼬리를 천천히 흔드는 이유는 균형을 잡기 위해서이다. 그런 개에게는 다가가지도 말고 웃지도 마라! 만약 웃게 되면 치아를 드러내게 될 것이고, 개는 그것을 자기에게 공격하려는 뜻으로 받아들일 것이다. 몸을 옆으로 살짝 틀고 (등을 완전히 보이면 안 된다) 부드러운 목소리로 말하면서 천천히 피한다.

2. ④ **Hello!** (안녕하세요!)

This is the human equivalent to a handshake. Social dogs will frequently and gently bite each other's collars in a similar manner. This is a dog's way of saying, "Hello."

이것은 인간의 악수와 같다. 비슷한 방식으로, 사교성이 풍부한 개들끼리는 서로의 목덜미를 자주 살짝 물기도 한다. 이것은 개가 인사하는 한 방법이다.

3. ③ **I am submissive. I give up!** (항복! 내가 졌어요!)

This dog is saying that he is submissive. He is saying that he is sorry for what he has done to anger you. Don't make the mistake of punishing the dog, because this will lead to a reoccurrence of the same behavior.

이 개는 절대 복종하겠다는 의사 표시를 하고 있다. 자신의 행동으로 당신을 화나게 한 것에 대해 용서를 구하고 있다. 이때 절대로 개를 벌하는 실수를 저지르지 않도록 한다. 벌을 주면 같은 행동을 반복할 것이기 때문이다.

4. ④ **He wants to show the other dog who is boss.** (당신의 개는 다른 개에게 누가 주도권을 쥐고 있는지 보여주기를 원한다.)

Although you may think your dog is confused or can't seem to distinguish between male and female, this is wrong. This behavior is all about dominance. It is a common site for male dogs to mount other male dogs as well as for females, to do the same.

만약 당신의 개가 수컷인지 암컷인지 혼동하거나 구별하지 못한다고 생각하면 그것은 오산이다. 이 행동은 주도권에 관한 것이다. 암컷이나 수컷끼리 올라타는 것은 흔한 행동이다.

5. ② I am nervous. (지금 떨려요.)

A common behavioral characteristic in nervous dogs is that they yawn. Of course, animals yawn when they are tired. Before judging the situation, you should take into consideration the environment in which the behavior exists. Dogs also yawn to show contentment.

개가 긴장했을 때 흔히 보이는 행동이 하품이다. 물론 피곤할 때도 하품을 한다. 따라서 하품하는 이유를 판단하기에 앞서 그 행동이 일어나는 상황을 고려해야 할 것이다. 만족감을 표시하기 위해 하품을 하는 경우도 있다.

6. ① I need a break. (좀 쉬어야겠어요.)

When a dog is scratching and shaking like he is wet when he isn't, then the dog is displaying that there is currently too much for him to deal with. Your dog is overloaded with information. Your dog needs a rest to calm down.

개가 목을 심하게 긁거나 젖지도 않았는데 젖었을 때처럼 몸을 턴다면, 그것은 현재 하고 있는 일이 힘들다는 것을 보여준다. 당신의 개에게 지나치게 많은 정보를 주고 있는 것이다. 당신의 개는 마음을 가라앉히기 위해 휴식이 필요하다.

7. ② I surrender! I am sorry! (내가 졌어요! 잘못했어요!)

Your dog is expressing that he does not want to challenge you and your leadership. He recognizes that you are the boss. He is saying that he is sorry. If your dog is submissive, he will never stare at you for a long period. Never punish your pet for this behavior. He is acknowledging that you are the boss and master. This is also true with other dogs.

당신의 개는 당신에게 도전하고 싶지 않으며 당신의 지시를 따르겠다는 표시를 하고 있다. 그는 당신이 주인이라는 사실을 인정하고 있다. 잘못했다고 용서를 구하고 있는 것이다. 절대 복종하겠다는 생각을 하면 당신을 오랫동안 똑바로 쳐다보지 못한다. 이미 당신이 주인이라는 사실을 인식하고 있으므로, 당신을 피한다고 혼내지 않도록 한다. 다른 개들도 마찬가지이다.

8. ③ I am afraid of you. I may bite or run. (당신이 무서워서 물거나 도망갈지도 몰

These are the general characteristics that are associated with a dog that is afraid. These dogs tend to be the most dangerous, because they are biting you to protect themselves. The flat turned ear of the dog indicates fear. In most cases, a dog will run or escape, but if he is cornered, he will often attack aggressively. In such a situation, the best thing to do is coax the dog to you. Don't just run up to him and assume that he wants to play. Do not approach such an animal with a smile! If you smile, you might show your teeth, and a dog will understand this as aggression.

개는 무서워할 때 이러한 증상을 보인다. 이러한 개들이 제일 위험하다. 왜냐하면 자신을 보호하기 위해 당신을 물지도 모르기 때문이다. 귀가 납작하게 뒤로 붙어 있으면 그것은 개가 두려워하고 있다는 표시이다. 대부분의 경우 개들은 도망가지만, 궁지에 몰렸다는 생각이 들면 공격적인 성향을 띤다. 만약 그러한 경우라면, 잘 달래 당신에게 오도록 한다. 개가 놀아 달라는 것으로 생각해 곧장 개에게 다가가면 안 된다. 그런 개에게는 웃으며 접근하지 마라! 만약 이를 드러내 보이면 개는 당신이 공격할 것이라고 여기기 때문이다.

9. ④ I smell a female dog in heat. (발정기 암컷의 냄새를 맡았어요.)

Before dogs mate, there is a courtship process where the male dog bites and nibbles on the female dog's ears. Your dog is excited and is preparing for that. Doctors also speculate that this behavior may increase the dog's ability to smell.

발정기에 개들은 짝짓기에 앞서 구애를 한다. 수컷들은 암컷들의 귀를 물거나 자근자근 깨문다. 당신의 개는 흥분한 상태이며, 짝짓기 준비가 되어 있는 것이다. 수의사들은 이러한 행동이 냄새를 맡는 개의 능력을 증진시킨다고 생각한다.

10. ③ Please play with me. (나와 놀아 주세요.)

These are all common behaviors exhibited by a dog that wants to play.

같이 놀아 달라고 할 때 흔히 보이는 행동이다.

48 The Top 5 Most Intelligent Dog Breeds

가장 영리한 5대 품종

Which breed of dog is the smartest? How can we measure a dog's intelligence? These two questions are at the center of an ongoing controversial debate over dog intelligence. Some experts argue that a dog's intelligence is to be measured by the amount of time it takes the canine to learn a command. Others argue that a dog's intelligence should be measured by the dog's independent ability to solve problems. There are 701 types of recognized pure breed dogs. These breeds are divided into seven different groups: 1. Toys, 2. Hounds, 3. Herding, 4. Sporting, 5. Terrier, 6. Non-Sporting, 7. Working.

어떤 품종의 개가 가장 영리할까? 개의 지능은 어떻게 측정할까? 이 두 가지 질문은 개의 지능을 둘러싼 논란의 핵심이다. 일부 전문가들은 개의 지능은 훈련 때 명령을 숙지하는 데 드는 소요 시간을 기준으로 측정되어야 한다고 하는 반면, 다른 전문가들은 독자적으로 문제를 해결할 수 있는 능력을 기준으로 측정되어야 한다고 주장한다. 전세계에는 701가지의 순종이 존재한다. 이들 품종을 다음의 7가지 그룹으로 분류할 수 있다: 1. 애완견, 2. 하운드(사냥견), 3. 축산 보조견, 4. 스포츠견, 5. 테리어(사냥견), 6. 비스포츠견, 7. 사역견.

The ratings below are for the Working/Obedience Intelligence of dogs. They are breed dependent and based on the following:

개들의 일 수행 및 복종 능력을 토대로 순위를 정했다. 품종별로 분리했으며 다음 사항을 기준으로 삼았다.

① Understanding of New Commands: Less than 5 repetitions.
② Obey First Command: 95% of the time or better.

① 새로운 명령어 이해도: 5회 미만 반복으로 숙지 가능
② 한 번의 명령으로 복종: 95% 이상

Rank & Breed 순위　　품종	Group & Characteristics 그룹　　　　특징
1　Border Collie 보더콜리	**Herding Group** 축산 보조견 The Border Collie is lively, intelligent, keen, alert, and receptive. It is a diligent worker that is both affectionate towards friends and protective of loved ones. 보더콜리는 활달하고 영리하며 민첩하고 상대방을 잘 받아들인다. 보더콜리는 부지런한 일꾼으로 친구들에게 사랑스러운 행동을 보이며 사랑하는 사람을 보호한다.
2　Poodle 푸들	**Non-Sporting Group / Toy Group** 비스포츠견, 애완견 The most notable characteristic of the Poodle is that it carries himself about proudly, almost arrogantly. The Poodle is very active and highly intelligent. Poodles also tend to be sharp and sometimes shy. 푸들의 가장 두드러지는 특징은 자신감에 넘친다는 것이다. 거만을 떠는 것처럼 보일 정도이다. 푸들은 활동적이며 상당히 영리하다. 예민하고 수줍음을 타기도 한다.

Rank & Breed 순위 품종	Group & Characteristics 그룹 특징
3 German Shepherd 저먼셰퍼드	**Herding Group** 축산 보조견 The German Shepherd has distinct characteristics of fearlessness without hostility. German shepherds are brave, confident, and alert canines. German shepherds are excellent watchdogs and are frequently used to lead the blind. 저먼 셰퍼드는 두려움이 없으면서도 적대적이지 않다. 저먼셰퍼드는 용감하고 자신감에 넘치며 민첩하다. 또한 뛰어난 경비견이며 맹인견으로도 활동한다.
4 Golden Retriever 골든리트리버	**Sporting Group** 스포츠견 This breed has distinct temperaments of being friendly, reliable, and trustworthy. Golden Retrievers are agile, eager, alert dogs, which are always hard working. Golden Retrievers are primarily used for hunting. 골든리트리버는 상냥하고 믿음직스럽다. 골든리트리버는 민첩하고 활동적이며 힘든 일도 마다하지 않는다. 주로 사냥견으로 이용된다.
5 Doberman Pinscher 도베르만핀셔	**Working Group** 사역견 The Doberman Pinschers are an energetic, noble, watchful, alert, fearless, loyal and obedient canine. These dogs are graceful in appearance, yet muscular and powerful. They are excellent watchdogs and possess great speed as well as endurance. 도베르만핀셔는 에너지가 넘치고 고고해 보이며, 민첩하고, 두려움이 없으며 복종한다. 도베르만핀셔는 외모가 우아하면서도 근육이 탄탄하고 힘이 세다. 따라서 경비견으로 손색이 없다. 지구력과 함께 스피드도 갖추고 있다.

개와 인간의 수명 비교

Although you love and care for your pet dearly, the chances are that if you were a dog owner, you would experience a loss and outlive your pet. There are several age comparison charts available on the Internet. However, this age chart was obtained from "The Pet's Friend," a reputable veterinarian clinic located in Sunnyvale, California. This chart should be used as a general reference.

애완견을 아무리 사랑한다고 해도 만약 당신이 애완견을 기르고 있다면 애완견을 먼저 떠나보내야 할 경우가 생길 수도 있을 것이다. 인터넷을 검색하다 보면 인간과 개의 수명 비교표가 많이 나와 있지만, 이 표는 캘리포니아 서니베일에 소재한 유명한 동물병원으로부터 입수한 것이다. 이 표는 일반적인 참고용으로만 사용해야 한다.

Dog's Age 개의 나이		Human Years 인간의 나이	
6 months	6개월	10 years	10세
8 months	8개월	13 years	13세
10 months	10개월	14 years	14세
12 months	12개월	15 years	15세
18 months	18개월	20 years	20세
2 years	2세	22 years	22세
4 years	4세	32 years	32세
6 years	6세	40 years	40세
8 years	8세	48 years	48세
10 years	10세	56 years	56세
12 years	12세	64 years	64세
14 years	14세	72 years	72세
16 years	16세	80 years	80세
18 years	18세	88 years	88세
20 years	20세	96 years	96세
21 years	21세	100 years	100세

50 Year of the Dog

개의 해

According to the traditional Korean and Chinese calendars, people born in the Year of the Dog possess the best [1]traits of human nature. Dogs are thought to be loyal, [2]diplomatic, [3]trustworthy, and [4]dutiful by people. They are excellent friends. They are rather intelligent and [5]selfless, but they can also be withdrawn at times and seem defensive and [6]stubborn.

Dogs are known for speaking sharply and then later regretting it. Always ready to help and to be fair to those around them, dogs also make good leaders. Dogs are thought to get along best with horses, rabbits, and tigers.

If you were born in one of the following years, you were born during the Year of the Dog:

1910 1922 1934 1946 1958 1970 1982 1994 2006 2018 2030

Below is an alphabetical list of some of the more famous people born in the Year of the Dog.

Andre Agassi, David Bowie, Buddha, George W. Bush, Winston Churchill, Bill Clinton, Confucius, Benjamin

Franklin, Judy Garland, J. Edgar Hoover, Michael
Jackson, Jennifer Lopez, Sophia Loren, Madonna, Dolly
Parton, Elvis Presley, Claudia Shiffer, Norman
Schwarzkopf, Socartes, Steven Spielberg, Sylvester
Stallone, Donald Trump.

1 trait 성격, 습관의 특징 **2 diplomatic** 외교의, 외교 수완이 있는 **3 trustworthy** 신뢰[신용]할 수 있는 **4 dutiful** 충실한, 순종하는 **5 selfless** 사심이 없는, 헌신적인 **6 stubborn** 완고한, 고집 센

한국과 중국의 전통 역법에 따르면, 개의 해에 태어난 사람들은 최고의 품성을 지니고 있다. 개띠들은 충직하고 외교적 수완이 좋으며 신뢰할 수 있고 성실하다고 한다. 친구로서 더할 나위가 없는 사람들이다. 똑똑한 편인데다 이기적이지도 않지만, 가끔씩 움츠러들면서 방어적인 태도를 취하고 고집을 부리기도 한다.

개띠들은 생각 없이 상대방의 마음을 상하게 하는 말을 내뱉고 나서 후회하는 것으로 알려져 있다. 주위 사람들을 도와줄 만반의 준비를 하고 있으며 공정하다. 지도자로서의 자질도 갖추고 있다. 개띠들은 말, 토끼, 호랑이띠 사람들과 궁합이 잘 맞는다.

다음에 열거한 해에 태어났다면 당신은 개띠이다.

1910 1922 1934 1946 1958 1970 1982 1994 2006 2018 2030

다음은 개의 해에 태어난 유명 인사들을 알파벳 순서로 정리한 것이다.

안드레 아가시, 데이비드 보위, 싯다르타 고타마(부처), 조지 부시, 윈스턴 처칠, 빌 클린턴, 공자, 벤자민 프랭크린, 주디 갈런드, 존 에드거 후버, 마이클 잭슨, 제니퍼 로페즈, 소피아 로렌, 마돈나, 돌리 파턴, 엘비스 프레슬리, 클라우디아 쉬퍼, 노먼 슈워츠코프, 소크라테스, 스티븐 스필버그, 실베스터 스탤런, 도널드 트럼프.

Below is a comprehensive alphabetized list of the 46 most commonly used dog idioms and expressions. Each idiom has been translated into Korean, and an example sentence has been provided for further reference as to how the idiom is used.

가장 많이 사용되는 개와 관련된 숙어 및 관용적인 표현 46가지를 알파벳 순서로 정리하고 그 의미와 예문을 곁들였다. 해석도 함께 실었다.

5

Dog Idiomatic Expressions

'dog'가 들어가는 관용적 표현

관용어구

as mean as a junkyard dog: very mean, vicious, or cross. 성질이 나쁘고 고약한, 다루기 힘든

The army drill instructor seemed to be *as mean as a junkyard dog.* He barked and screamed orders all day.
훈련 교관은 성질이 고약해 보였다. 그는 하루종일 고함을 질러댔다.

as sick as a dog: very sick. 몸의 컨디션이 매우 나쁜, 감기가 심한

Erin stayed home from school yesterday, because she was *as sick as a dog.*
에린은 어제 너무 아파서 학교에 가지 않고 집에 있었다.

bark up the wrong tree: to waste one's time and efforts by pursuing or taking the wrong course of action. 헛다리짚다, 엉뚱한 사람을 추적하다

If you think that I have your wallet, you're *barking up the wrong tree.*
네 지갑을 내가 가지고 있다고 생각한다면 헛다리짚은 거야.

call off the dogs: to stop following or pursuing someone; to stop using hound dogs to find the scent of someone. 추적을 멈추다

Due to the weather conditions, the police were forced to *call off the dogs.*
기상 상황 때문에 경찰은 추적을 중단할 수밖에 없었다.

die a dog's death: to die a terrible, dreadful death. 비참하게 죽다

It is said that early travelers to the remote island *died a dog's death* at the hands of the island tribe members.

180

그 외딴 섬의 초기 여행객들은 섬의 원주민들에게 비참한 죽음을 당했다고 한다.

dirty dog: a terrible person; a person of no morals. 망나니, 못된 사람

When I find the *dirty dog* that stole my wallet, I'm going to turn him in to the police.

내 지갑을 훔친 그 못된 놈을 찾기만 하면 경찰에 넘길 거야.

dog: someone who is ugly; a very impolite expression that describes an ugly woman. 못생긴 사람, 추녀

Gross! I would never kiss her. She is a *dog*!

맙소사! 그녀와 절대로 키스하지 않을 거야. 그녀는 너무 못생겼어.

dog and pony show: an impressive show or performance to impress someone, like a boss or superior. 사장이나 상급자에게 좋은 인상을 주기 위해 노력하는 것

Our regional manager will be visiting the office next Friday so we will have to put on a *dog and pony show* for him.

지역 간부가 다음주 금요일에 사무실을 방문할 예정이기 때문에 그에게 좋은 인상을 주기 위해 노력해야 한다.

dog days of summer: the very hot days in July and August. 한여름의 매우 더운 날씨, 삼복

During the *dog days of summer,* it is best to drink lots of fluids and stay out of the sun.

여름의 찌는 듯한 더운 날씨에는 수분을 많이 섭취하고 햇빛을 피하는 게 최고야.

dog-eared: having been used so much that the corners of the pages of a book are turned down or torn. 책장 모서리가 접힌, 사용해서 낡은

Cindy borrowed my new book, but when she returned it, it was *dog-eared.*

신디는 내 새 책을 빌려갔는데, 돌려줄 때 보니까 책이 너덜너덜했다.

dog-eat-dog: ruthlessly acquisitive or competitive; a rough, ruthless competition. 치열하게 다투는, 인정사정없는; 치열한 경쟁, 골육상쟁

Life and job searching after graduation seems to be *dog-eat-dog.*

졸업 후의 생존 경쟁과 취업 경쟁은 정말로 치열하다.

dog-faced liar: a terrible liar. 심한 거짓말쟁이.

I don't trust him. I think that he is a *dog-faced liar*.
나는 그를 신뢰할 수 없어. 그는 정말 심한 거짓말쟁이야.

dog in the manger: someone who prevents others from enjoying something even though one has no use for it. 이기적이고 심술 사나운 사람, 자기에게 필요 없는 것도 남 주기 아까워 방해하는 심술쟁이(이솝우화에서)

Why are you being a *dog in the manger*? If you are not going to the movie, give the tickets to someone who can go.
왜 그렇게 심술을 부려? 극장에 가지 않을 거면 갈 수 있는 사람에게 입장권을 줘.

dog-leg right *or* dog-leg left: fairway turns in a golf course. 골프 코스 중 왼쪽[오른쪽]으로 꺾어진 홀

Harry advised me to be careful during my next golf shot, because the fairway was a *dog-leg left*.
해리는 페어웨이가 왼쪽으로 꺾어져 있으니 샷을 날릴 때 조심하라고 조언했다.

Dog my cats: an expression that one makes when surprised, like "Oh my goodness!" 앳! (놀람을 나타내는 소리)

Dog my cats! You scared me! Don't do that again.
앗! 놀랐잖아! 다시는 그러지 마.

dog paddle: a basic type of swimming stroke; to swim an elementary stroke imitating a swimming dog. 개헤엄(치다)

Most young swimmers learn how to *dog paddle* before they learn harder swimming strokes.
대부분의 어린 수영 선수들은 난이도 높은 영법을 익히기 전에 개헤엄부터 배운다.

dog's life: a terribly miserable and unhappy existence. 비참한 생활

Sometimes I think that I am leading a *dog's life*. Working in a factory all day is nothing bright in my future.
가끔 나는 내가 정말 비참한 생활을 한다고 생각한다. 미래에 대한 아무런 희망도 없이 공장에서 하루 종일 일하니 말이다.

the dogs of war: the sick crushing calamity of war. 전쟁의 참화

During the Vietnam War, ordinary people caught a glimpse of *the dogs of war* through media reports and camera footage.

베트남전쟁 동안 보통 사람들은 신문 방송의 보도를 통해 전쟁의 참혹함을 엿볼 수 있었다.

dog tag: a small metal tag containing identifying information worn around the necks of military service members; an identifying metal tag that is worn around a dog's neck. 군인의 인식표; 개목걸이

As soon as Tim became a member of the army, he was handed *dog tags* and told never to take them off.

팀은 입대하자마자 인식표를 받았고 절대로 빼지 말라는 명령을 들었다.

dog-tired: very tired. 매우 지친, 녹초가 된

After working for fourteen hours on the farm, Dan was *dog-tired* and went to sleep without taking a shower.

댄은 농장에서 14시간을 일한 후 녹초가 되어 샤워도 하지 않은 채 잠이 들었다.

Every dog has its day: there will be a time in everyone's life when he or she is successful and able to exhibit influence or power over others. 쥐구멍에도 볕들 날이 있다.

Your future may not seem bright now, but remember, *every dog has its day*.

현재로서는 너의 미래가 밝아 보이지 않는다고 해도 쥐구멍에도 볕들 날이 있다는 사실을 명심해라.

fight like cats and dogs: to fight violently all the time. 자주 심하게 싸우다

The young newly married couple seemed to *fight like cats and dogs* during the first six months of their marriage.

젊은 신혼부부는 결혼 후 처음 6개월 동안 자주 심하게 다투는 것 같았다.

gone to the dogs: for something to have taken a turn for the worse. 몰락하다, 파멸하다

Albert's plan to lose weight has *gone to the dogs*. He has

gained more weight than he lost.

살을 빼려는 앨버트의 계획은 실패로 돌아갔다. 살을 빼기는커녕 오히려 더 쪘다.

hair of the dog that bit you: the root of your illness used as a remedy or a cure, especially for alcohol related hangovers. 치료약을 병의 원인에서 찾아내는 것, 숙취를 술로써 해결함

I think that I need a little *hair of the dog that bit me* to cure this terrible hangover that I have.

이 지독한 숙취는 술로 해결해야 할 것 같아.

His bark is worse than his bite: an expression used when a person seems to be more aggressive or intimidating than he or she actually is. 그(녀)의 본성은 보기와 달리 나쁘지 않다.

Don't worry about Mark. *His bark is worse than his bite.* Once you get to know him, you'll find that he is one of the nicest people that you'll ever meet.

마크에 대해서는 걱정하지 마. 그의 본성은 보기와 달리 나쁘지 않거든. 일단 그를 알게 되면, 정말 좋은 사람이라는 것을 너도 느끼게 될 거야.

hot dog: a person that executes skillful sports movements precisely to draw attention from others. 스포츠에서 묘기를 가진 사람

Dan is a real *hot dog*! He can do the hardest snowboarding moves better than anyone!

댄은 진짜 출중해! 고난도 스노보딩에서 그를 이길 자는 없을 거야!

If you lie down with dogs, you will get up with fleas: You will acquire the faults of bad people if you associate with them. 까마귀 노는 곳에 백로야 가지 마라.

Steven's father warned Steven to stay away from the older group of rough-looking teenagers by saying, *"If you lie down with dogs, you will get up with fleas."*

스티븐의 아버지는 '까마귀 노는 곳에 백로야 가지 마라' 는 속담을 인용하면서 스티븐에게 다소 거칠어 보이는 10대 상급생 무리들에서 빠져 나오라고 했다.

in the doghouse: in trouble. 노여움을 사서, 면목을 잃고

Tom was *in the doghouse* with his wife after drinking with his friends and returning home at 3:00 am.
톰은 친구들과 술 마시고 새벽 3시에 귀가한 후 아내의 눈치를 보며 쩔쩔매고 있었다.

It's a dog eat dog world: It's a vicious cruel world. 잔인한 세상이다; 지독한 세상이다.

Before leaving home, Darren's father told him, "*It's a dog eat dog world,* so be careful."
대런이 집을 나서기 전에 그의 아버지는 "무서운 세상이니 조심하거라."고 당부했다.

Let sleeping dogs lie: Don't bring up issues or topics that will raise tempers or cause arguments. 잠자는 개를 건드리지 마라; 긁어 부스럼 만들지 마라.

Son, I know that you put a dent in the car, and I think we should just get it fixed without telling your father. It is best to *let sleeping dogs lie*.
애야, 네가 차를 찌그러뜨린 건 아는데, 아빠에게는 말씀 드리지 말고 우리끼리 고치도록 하자. 괜히 긁어 부스럼 만들지 않는 게 상책이야.

like a dog with two tails: very happy. 매우 기쁜

Martin acted *like a dog with two tails* when he received the new computer program that he wanted for his birthday.
마틴은 생일 선물로 바라던 새로운 컴퓨터 프로그램을 받게 되자 뛸 듯이 기뻤다.

like a dog's dinner: being dressed smartly or ostentatiously. 멋지게[화려하게] 옷을 차려입은

Wow! Look at Jeff! He is dressed *like a dog's dinner*.
와! 제프 좀 봐, 쫙 빼 입었네.

look like someone just shot one's dog: to look terribly upset or troubled. 당황한 표정을 짓다

Something is wrong with Jay. He *looks like someone just shot his dog*.
제이에게 무언가 일이 생긴 것 같다. 표정이 안 좋아.

Love me, love my dog: If you love someone, you should accept everything about that person, including their faults. 나를 사랑한다면 나의 모든 것을 사랑해라, 단점까지도.

When Joe asked Karen to marry him, she responded by saying, *"Love me, love my dog."*
조가 청혼했을 때 캐런이 대답했다. "나를 사랑한다면 내 모든 것을 사랑해 주세요."

My dogs are barking: My feet are aching and hurting. 발이 아프다.

After a full day of door-to-door sales, Andy sighed as he took off his shoes and said, "Oh, *my dogs are barking.*"
하루 종일 방문 판매를 한 후에, 앤디는 신발을 벗으며 "아, 발 아파."라고 말했다.

put on the dog: to act or behave as if you are more elegant, extravagant, and important than you actually are. 잘난 체하다

I'll have to *put on the dog* next week when my mother-in-law visits for a few days.
장모가 며칠 묵게 될 다음주에는 잘난 체 좀 해야 한다.

rain cats and dogs: to rain very heavily. 비가 퍼붓다

It has been *raining cats and dogs* all day!
하루 종일 비가 퍼부었어!

see a man about a dog: to excuse oneself without giving the real reason for leaving, mainly to go to the toilet. (주로 화장실에 다녀올 때 다른 핑계를 대면서) 잠시 자리를 비우다

As Ryan stood up at the table, he said that he had to *see a man about a dog* and that he would return again shortly.
라이언은 테이블에서 일어서면서 잠시 자리를 비웠다가 곧 돌아오겠다고 말했다.

shaggy dog story: an overly long joke with a ridiculously silly or meaningless ending. 엉뚱한 결말의 황당하고 매우 긴 이야기

Todd's *shaggy dog story* seemed to spoil the mood at the dinner table so much that many people just kept quiet throughout the rest of the evening.
토드의 썰렁하고 지루한 이야기는 식사 분위기를 완전히 망가뜨려 사람들은 남은 저녁 시간 내

내 침묵만 지킬 뿐이었다.

the tail wagging the dog: a small or unimportant factor or element governing an important one; a reversal of the proper roles. 작은 일부가 전체를 조종하는 상황, 주객전도

It was quite a case of *the tail wagging the dog* when Tammy explained Egyptian history to her high school history teacher.
태미가 이집트 역사에 대해 그녀의 역사 선생님에게 설명할 때 완전히 주객이 전도된 것 같았다.

throw something to the dogs: to give something up; to throw something away. 내버리다, 희생시키다

Parents need to prepare their children for life after graduation. They simply can't just *throw their children to the dogs* without preparing them first.
부모들은 자녀들이 졸업한 뒤의 인생에 대해 준비시킬 필요가 있다. 무방비 상태로 그들을 세상에 내보내서는 안 된다.

top dog: the best or most important one; number one. 가장 훌륭한[중요한] 사람

Mark is the *top dog* in our archery club. Nobody can beat him when he tries his best.
마크는 우리 양궁 클럽에서 최고다. 그가 최선을 다하면 누구도 그를 당할 수가 없다.

treat someone like a dog: to treat someone cruelly or savagely. 잔혹하게 대하다

When my old boss started to *treat all of the employees like dogs*, most of them quit and began to look for jobs elsewhere.
우리 사장이 직원들을 박정하게 대하기 시작하자, 그들은 대부분 사표를 내고 다른 직장을 알아보기 시작했다.

underdog: a person or team that is expected to lose a contest or struggle, as in sports or politics. 패배가 예상되는 사람[팀]

Even though our team was the *underdog*, we beat the other team easily.

우리 팀의 패배가 예상되었는데도 불구하고 우리는 상대 팀을 쉽게 이겼다.

work like a dog: to work very hard. 몸을 아끼지 않고 열심히 일하다

During a hot summer day, my friends and I *worked like dogs* to help my father repair the roof.

무더운 여름날 나와 내 친구들은 우리 아버지가 지붕을 고칠 때 몸을 아끼지 않고 열심히 도왔다.

You can't teach an old dog new tricks: It is very difficult to teach new skills or change longstanding habits or character traits in people. 새로운 기술을 가르치거나 사람의 성격[습관]을 바꾸기란 매우 어렵다.

I tried to show my father how to use the computer, but *you can't teach an old dog new tricks.*

아버지에게 컴퓨터 사용법을 가르치려고 했지만, 구세대에게 새로운 방법을 가르치는 것은 정말 어려운 일이다.

The Author's Recommendation

부록: 애완견 관련 사이트

Below is a list of author-recommended sites for you to visit. Each site offers interesting information along with additional links for you and your dog.

다음은 필자가 추천하는 인터넷 사이트 목록이다. 이들 추천 사이트를 활용하면 개에 관한 흥미로운 정보를 수집할 수 있을 뿐만 아니라 다양한 관련 사이트가 링크되어 있다.

Recommended Web Sites

www.akc.org

Detailed information about dog breeds and behavior.

개의 품종 및 행태에 대한 자세한 정보 수록.

www.dogbreedinfo.com

Information on dog breeds, mixed breeds, dog stories, and classifieds.

개의 품종, 잡종, 개 이야기, 안내 광고.

www.dog-play.com

Great games, activities, and tricks to play with and teach to your dog. This site provides detailed explanations and categories for each activity.

개 훈련 및 놀이에 효과적인 게임, 활동, 트릭. 각 활동에 대해 카테고리별로 자세한 설명 수록.

www.nextdaypets.com

A complete site for dog lovers that includes dog breeders, pet supplies, puppies for sale, and a comprehensive list of pet and dog friendly hotels.

애견인들에게 유용한 사이트. 애견 사육자, 애견용품 업체, 분양견, 애완동물에게 우호적인 호텔 목록.

www.vetinfo.com

An online Veterinary Information Service for both dogs and cats. This site includes a detailed canine medical encyclopedia filled with volumes of information.

개와 고양이를 위한 온라인 수의학 관련 정보. 방대한 정보가 실린 수의학 백과사전 제공.

www.cleanrun.com

Dog accessories for the serious owner, dedicated to improving their pet's agility and physical endurance.

애완동물의 민첩성 및 지구력 향상에 관심이 지대한 애견 주인을 위한 애완동물 용품 소개.

www.animaljobs.com

A detailed website of animal jobs, jobs working with animals, veterinary jobs, pet stores, and more. For people who love working with animals.

동물을 돌보는 직업, 동물과 함께 일하는 직업, 동물 병원 관련 직업, 애완동물 매장 등에 대한 자세한 소개. 동물과 함께 일하기를 원하는 사람들에게 유용한 사이트.

www.thepetprofessor.com

A dog and pet site filled with useful links related to dog and pet ownership. This site includes links to Pet Forums where you can communicate with other pet owners online.

애완견을 비롯한 애완동물 소유와 관련된 많은 유용한 사이트가 링크되어 있는 사이트. 다른 애완동물 주인들과 온라인으로 채팅할 수 있는 펫 포럼과도 링크된다.

www.cooldogtoys.com

This site is filled with dog toys and interesting accessories hard to find elsewhere.

다른 곳에서는 쉽게 찾을 수 없는 개 장난감과 흥미로운 애견용품 소개.

www.aphis.usda.gov/vs/sregs/

U.S. State & Territory Animal Import Regulations — Before you ship an animal or move to the US with your pet, you should check regulations regarding the import of animals.

미국 동물 반입 규정 수록. 애완동물 등을 미국으로 데려갈 경우 동물 반입 규제를 사전에 반드시 확인한다.

일러스트 **김은정**

서울대 미대 서양화과를 졸업하고 (주)바른손에서 디자이너로 근무했다.
이후 출판 일러스트레이션에 관심을 갖고 프리랜스 일러스트레이터로
일하면서 일반 단행본과 동화책 등에 예쁜 일러스트를 많이 그려 넣고 있다.

Dog English

초판 1쇄 발행 2007년 3월 10일

지은이 매튜 다우마
펴낸이 엄경희
펴낸곳 서프라이즈

주소 서울시 마포구 도화동 173 삼창빌딩 1403호
전화 02) 719-9758 팩스 02) 719-9768
이메일 surprise@surprisepub.co.kr
등록 2003년 12월 20일 제 313-2003-00382호

ISBN 978-89-955053-7-3 13740

값 12,000원